# ENDORSEMENTS

Every Christian in the business world struggles with a variety of daily issues. Reneé offers her life as an open book to all who struggle with these difficult matters. Share her journey through worry, success, pain, triumph, defeat, and content. To one degree or another, we all face those same struggles. This true–life story is definitely worth the read for anyone facing tough, daily business decisions.

—Steve Hemphill, business owner and author of
*My Search for the Real Heaven*

Reneé's experiences will minister to many souls and let them know that they are not the only ones in the fire and in their situations. The good news is that you *will* come through that fire, refined and pure as gold with Jesus standing right there with you, having never left you or forsaken you.

—Chris Chitwood, president of Dialog
Wireline Services, LLC

# God's Hands
## *in My*
# BUSINESS

Best Wishes!
Renee' Meaux
2011

Reneé Meaux

# God's Hands
## *in My*
# BUSINESS

*Will He Let My Business Fail?*

TATE PUBLISHING & *Enterprises*

Published by Tate Publishing & Enterprises, LLC
127 E. Trade Center Terrace | Mustang, Oklahoma 73064 USA
1.888.361.9473 | www.tatepublishing.com

Tate Publishing is committed to excellence in the publishing industry. The company reflects the philosophy established by the founders, based on Psalm 68:11,
*"The Lord gave the word and great was the company of those who published it."*

Book design copyright © 2009 by Tate Publishing, LLC. All rights reserved.
*Cover design by Amber Gulilat*
*Interior design by Lindsay B. Behrens*

Published in the United States of America

ISBN: 978-1-60799-663-7
1. Religion / Christian Life / Professional Growth
2. Business & Economics / Entrepreneurship
09.06.29

This book is dedicated to my husband, Joey, and my two sons, Taylor and Alex. These three men have brought unimaginable joy to my life. I am so proud of each of them. I have been truly blessed.

I would also like to dedicate it to our family and friends who are so dear to our hearts. Thanks to each one of you for your love and support as we went through this time in our lives. Thank you for putting up with us. We could not have done it without you.

# TABLE OF CONTENTS

# PLANS TO TAKE
# THE EASY ROUTE

It isn't easy to bare your soul, to let your life be an open book for the world to read. The easiest thing would be to let the past stay right where it is, in the past. Why risk being the object of judgment and gossip? The past can be embarrassing, humiliating, and is better buried. We shouldn't (and can't accurately) judge people unless we've been in their shoes, but people do, even Christians.

I believe people should share their experiences, good and bad. Someone, somewhere has gone through, or is going through, something similar. People need to know they are not alone. An experience not shared, or not learned from, is an experience wasted. As they say, hindsight is twenty/twenty. Looking back, I can see things so clearly. Maybe I can help someone who is just beginning her journey, or who may be in the middle of his journey, with no end in sight. God calls us to minister to others.

Praise be to the God and Father of our Lord
Jesus Christ, the Father of compassion and the
God of all comfort, who comforts us in all our
troubles, so that we can comfort those in any
trouble with the comfort we ourselves have
received from God.

2 Corinthians 1:3–4

We are met with many decisions and choices in
this life. Sometimes we make mistakes and choose
the wrong path. If we truly prayerfully consider our
options and ask for the Lord's guidance, which-
ever paths we take will lead us to our ultimate fate,
whether good or bad. God has a plan for us. "Many
are the plans in a man's heart, but it is the Lord's
purpose that prevails" (Proverbs 19:21).

As far back as I can remember, it seems like I
always had a goal, a plan for myself. In elementary
school I was walking down the hall one day, and the
principal pulled me aside. He asked me if I knew
that I had the highest grade in my class. I was over-
whelmed with pride. I liked that feeling, and I knew
from that moment on that I had a plan. I found out
that there was such a thing as salutatorian and valedictorian, and I made up my mind that I would be
one of them.

I was blessed with the ability to do well in school.
Learning came easy to me. I knew what it would

take to make the grade, and that's what I did—
nothing more and nothing less. I was very active in
high school. I was a majorette and spent a lot of time
practicing. I spent a lot of time just being a teenager
as well. I wasn't exactly a bookworm.

Graduation came, and I had done it. I was salutatorian. I wrote and gave my speech with pride on
graduation night. I remembered telling my drama
teacher that I would not need any experience in
public speaking. He reminded me of that after the
ceremony. I had pulled it off, but I was extremely
nervous. I had no intentions of ever doing it again.

Unlike other *intelligent* people, I really hadn't
looked much past that. That wasn't very smart. The
valedictorian went on to become a doctor. I didn't
have the desire to leave home and go off to a big uni-
versity. I applied for a scholarship to the local junior
college and received it. I moved into an apartment
with a long–time friend, worked nights in a retail
store, and went to school during the day. I guess I
got tired of having been so structured for so long. I
skipped classes frequently and ultimately quit going.
I remember my English teacher approached me and
tried diligently to talk me out of quitting. I had done
well, when I was there. I had my mind made up to
quit, so it was to no avail. I assured her I would come
back and finish one day. I just wanted some time
off.

I had another plan for myself. The largest company around was Texas Eastman Company. I had heard they paid well, even if you didn't have a degree. That was it. That was the place for me. I would take the easy route. I put in my application and began calling regularly. In the meantime, which spanned a few years, I worked a couple of office jobs and ended up working for a plastics company. I continued to call Texas Eastman.

One day, after I had been with the plastics company for almost a year, I got a call. I was so excited! Eastman offered me a job. After all those years, they finally offered me a job. I had been out of high school for ten years. The HR person was a man. I will never forget what he said. He said, "I was looking at your record. Do you realize how good your grades are?" I thought that question was a little strange, but it made me feel very proud. My grades had followed me.

I went to Eastman and took a physical and passed. I turned in my two-weeks' notice at my present job and couldn't believe what happened next. David, my boss, counter-offered. He praised my work and did not want to see me leave. I was flattered. He had been impressed with my work and appreciated me. He offered to pay for my college education if I would stay. I told him I was looking for a career and a place where I could advance. He told me that I could have a career there. He told me I would probably be running the place one day (halfheartedly, of course). He was running it himself.

I had the weekend to make my decision. I talked to everyone I could, seeking advice. Most everyone advised me to go to Eastman. I spent a lot of time in prayer and asked God to help me make the right decision. Much to my surprise, as well as everyone else's, I decided to stay where I was. I am probably one of the few people who have ever respectfully declined Eastman's offer. I just hoped I wasn't as crazy as everyone thought I was. David told me he could not pay what Eastman offered right away, but he promised I would get there. Money was important, but it wasn't the only thing to be considered. Someone appreciated me, and that made a big difference.

# GOD'S PLAN PREVAILS

Over the ten years since I had graduated from high school, I'd gone through a lot. I had been married and divorced. I suffered broken relationships and a broken spirit. I drifted away from the Lord. I rode the fence for a long time, knowing how I was supposed to live but not doing it. I knew I needed to make a change in my life.

I took David up on his offer and went back to school. I worked forty hours a week and went to school three nights a week. This time, I was going to do what I knew I was capable of. There was no more skipping class. No grade below an A would be acceptable. I was going to make a life for myself, but this time it was all thanks to the Lord. I was no longer making decisions on my own. I didn't deserve his help, but he had not forsaken me.

I was twenty-nine and in college, with braces on my teeth. I was just a late bloomer. I had sought security and stability in relationships in my life but found neither. I was more determined than ever to be independent. I dated a few people off and on, but

I was not searching for another marriage partner. I just wanted to work on myself.

I worked hard and studied hard. I spent my free time with my friends who lived in my neighborhood. I made a friend at work as well. A new guy had come to our office. His name was Joey Meaux. I thought his name was very strange. *Meaux* is not common in Texas. He was from Louisiana. It's very common there.

Joey had previously worked for a customer of ours then came to work for us. He needed a place to live, so I told him about an empty duplex in my neighborhood. He moved in on the other side of my friends who lived a couple of streets down. They took him in as they had me. They frequently invited us both over for supper. We ended up spending a lot of time together and became good friends. He once told me he had thought about asking me out, but I just had all those rubber bands in my mouth. I was still wearing braces and virtually had my mouth sealed shut with rubber bands. I didn't mind being teased. I knew I would be proud of my new smile one day. Everything means more when you have to pay for it yourself. I thought he was cute, but I couldn't marry someone with the last name *Meaux*.

I continued to work my way up in the plastics company. I was promoted to accounting manager. Joey eventually became my best friend. We started dating and going to church together. He was born and raised in the Catholic church. I was born and raised in the Church of Christ. It never seemed to matter. We both liked my church and the preacher there. We had similar beliefs and dreams. It was actually odd how much alike yet different we were. We thought alike about most everything. On the other hand, he was more reserved than I was. We had a good relationship. Dating someone from work is usually risky business, but it worked well for us. The only time it could have been a serious problem was the day we stood and watched our plant burn down.

A fire had started on a Saturday afternoon, not long after Joey had left from a supervisor's meeting. Everyone made it out of the building except Margaret. Margaret could not be found, but her car was still in the parking lot. We were notified of the fire and rushed to the scene. We wanted to think that Margaret could possibly be somewhere else, but we knew deep down that it wasn't true. She worked in customer service, and her office was in the back of the building. They said the fumes from the burning plastic were poisonous. The fumes probably reached her before the fire did.

We stood by in horror as the flames engulfed our plant. Things like this happened to other people, not us. Losing our friend was a terrible experience. We also had to worry about both being unemployed. The business didn't skip a beat, though. The next day, all of the employees, including Joey and me, were at the scene again. We moved everything that was salvageable to an empty building next door. We conducted business there until we leased another place. We had an extravagant new building built in another location.

Joey and I mourned the loss of Margaret and attended her funeral together. That was just the beginning of our journey as a couple. At one point, I decided I was not going to have another marriage, and I broke it off. We were apart for about a week. The next thing you know, we were planning a wedding.

All along I felt as if I was living my life in third person. It was an out–of–body experience. That wasn't really me about to get married again. Something was pushing me forward, even though my mind wanted to scream at me to stop. I prayed about it, and I felt God calling. Something told me this time was different. This time I was marrying my best friend. This time I understood what unconditional love was. I understood that love was a decision and not an emotion.

We were married on a picturesque lake lot behind a friend's house. The weather was beautiful. A mutual friend, whom we had met at work, married us. He was a customer of ours and an ordained minister. We had a crawfish boil afterward. Joey's father brought the crawfish from Louisiana and boiled it for us. All of our family and friends were there. We went to Puerto Vallarta, Mexico, for our honeymoon that same week.

When we returned from our honeymoon, we started our new life together the best way we knew how. We went to the church on a Thursday evening and were baptized together. Joey and I both had made so many mistakes along the way. This was our way of asking for forgiveness and recommitting our lives, our marriage, to the Lord. I had been baptized at a very young age, but I couldn't think of a better way to start our journey together before God. I knew I wanted to put God first in my life. We both wanted to put God first.

We wanted to start a family as well. He was thirty–three, and I was thirty–one. I felt my biological clock ticking. To our surprise, it didn't take long at all. That week was a new beginning in more ways than one. I was pregnant within two weeks after we were married.

I continued to work and go to school. Joey began to work his way up in the company as well. We went to church regularly and prepared for our new baby. This would be the first child for both of us. We were very excited and scared of the unknown. I knew this was right. God knew all along that I wasn't meant to have children with anyone else. He blessed us with Taylor, a beautiful, healthy baby boy.

When Taylor was three months old, I walked across the stage and received my associate's degree. It had taken a long time going to night school. There were many exhausting late nights that I spent in tears because I was pregnant and wanted to sleep; but I had finally done it. I graduated with honors. My salary had more than doubled.

Joey and I began to make our dreams of a new home a reality. We were having a house built on some land directly behind my parents' house, the house I grew up in. Joey had moved into my small duplex because it was so inexpensive. We were saving money to build our home. The neighborhood we lived in had gone downhill. Our friends had all moved away and were replaced with less–than–law–abiding citizens. We were robbed, and our duplex was broken into twice. I was so ready to leave that place, but it had served its purpose. Our house was finished just in time for Taylor's first birthday.

# THE LORD PROVIDES

Things began to change at work. David decided to sell the company. The chief financial officer left because he suspected that the new owners would replace upper management. I was asked to take over his responsibilities and received another raise. Joey became the plant manager.

I absolutely hated working the corporate scene. The corporate office was in Chicago. Things were quite different there than what I had been accustomed to. I was forced to work very hard to keep up with the demands. I put in late hours while Joey took care of our child. I was constantly working on forecasting and budgeting, things that David hadn't required. We were one of sixteen plants that had been purchased by the same company.

I was the only one in my position who had a two–year degree. Most of the others were CPAs. I had to prove myself to keep the job. One of the Chicago CPAs befriended me. He taught me the things I needed to know. I was very thankful he was there to save me. Suddenly I didn't feel the security I had felt with David.

Our security blanket seemed to be ripped out from underneath us. The company was changing, and our lives were changing as well. I became pregnant with our second child. Joey's father became ill. Our second son, Alex, was born on Joey's father's birthday, three weeks after he passed away. While I was still at home on maternity leave, it was announced that our company was shutting down. We were dealing with losing Joey's father in an untimely death to cancer. We now had two small children to care for and a new home and were about to be unemployed.

The good news was that we were getting severance packages. They gave each of us a letter informing us how much we would receive. Joey would be receiving a pretty decent package. The bad news was that I would not be receiving what I should have gotten because I had been on maternity leave. They had hired someone to replace me while I was away, and he would be getting the full package.

Seven years I had given this company. My replacement had not been there two months. That was one of the few times in my life that I can remember feeling so wronged. I had spent countless nights on the job, giving one hundred percent to my employers. They could not have cared less. They were in Chicago. They didn't know me. I believed I was cheated out of fourteen weeks of pay, and it made me angry. I sought and found a lawyer who was willing to take my case. He was then intimidated by the team of lawyers representing the company and referred me to someone he believed would be more capable.

I had to return to work after my maternity leave was up in order to fulfill my obligations and receive the severance pay they were offering. During that time, I continued to do the best job I could do, although I had a very different attitude. I was allowed to leave early and let my replacement continue to do my responsibilities. Out of the kindness of their hearts, they offered to let me stay on until all of the assets had been transferred. That would be several months after the business closed. They were not happy with my replacement's work, but he would still receive the same severance package, and so would I. I was more than happy to leave and return home to my newborn child. It ended up being an extended maternity leave, more time than I ever would have imagined getting to spend with my children. It was a blessing in disguise.

A customer of ours had approached my husband and asked him to consider starting his own business. Several of our customers were not happy with the idea of transferring their business to Houston with the new company. Our friends we worked with were not happy about being unemployed. We were intrigued by the idea but didn't really think it was possible. We didn't think we would be capable of pulling it together.

Then we changed our way of thinking. The Lord is capable of anything. If we were willing to give him the chance, it might just happen. The experience I gained from working with the corporate office proved invaluable. I put together a three–year forecast and cash flow projection for our new business, based on existing realistic information. Joey put together a business plan. Together, with the Lord on our side, we were ready to seek funding. Before the doors of the plastics manufacturing company were closed, we had our new business plan in front of financial institutions and were looking for investors.

We made appointments with several venture capitalists in the area. Everyone seemed interested, but no one committed. It was by chance one day that we found our partners. We were having dinner in a restaurant one night. While we were there, we ran into my friend Connie and her husband, Gary, who joined us at our table. We told them what we were trying to do, and they were interested. They had been looking for something to invest in. We met and talked a few more times and came to an agreement. Then all we had to do was get the loan.

We spent our days and nights in constant prayer. I was still nursing my son and spent many nights praying in the dark, in my chair, at two o'clock in the morning. It was during that time that we decided to start tithing. We had always contributed money to the church but not ten percent. After hearing a sermon on tithing one Sunday, we decided to have faith and trust in God.

> Bring the whole tithe into the storehouse, that there may be food in my house. Test me in this, says the Lord Almighty, and see if I will not throw open the floodgates of heaven and pour out so much blessing that you will not have room enough for it.
>
> Malachi 3:10

We didn't know if we would be employed or not, but we believed the Lord would take care of us. This is the only place in the Bible where God says to test him. We were receiving unemployment payments along with the severance pay. The Lord was providing.

Not knowing how things would turn out, I began to look for other employment. I didn't really want to take another job, but I had received an offer I didn't think I should turn down. Everything was so uncertain. What if we didn't find a bank to give us a business loan? I couldn't sit around without work forever. The offer was one that might not come along again.

My new employer, Mark, was a Christian. That was a new and welcome experience for me. I liked and respected him. He was aware of what Joey and I had been trying to do and was supportive. I received some good advice from him and some more valuable experience from the job.

Joey had received severance pay for six months and had not worked. He had been looking also but had not found anything. Several banks had turned us down on the loan. It was looking doubtful. We were very involved with our church family, and we put ourselves on their prayer list. Even if we were able to get the loan, it would be a big load to carry. There were no guarantees that our endeavor would be successful. Everyone stood to lose a lot.

I left my job one day to go to lunch and heard something on the radio. The preacher was talking to me. It couldn't have been planned any better. He said that people miss out on the Lord's blessings because they are too afraid of risk. They don't believe they can achieve their goals. They lack trust and faith in God. The Lord thrives on doing the impossible. Our situation was certainly the impossible, so I decided I had one for him. It was then that I knew I was not afraid to go forward. If the Lord brought us a bank that was willing to loan the money, then I was certainly willing to give it my all.

One night it seemed *too* impossible. We had been turned down again, and there was only one bank left that was reviewing our information. The process had taken so many months that we stood to lose all our potential customers. Joey told me it was over. He told me I had better realize it and go on. But I didn't give up.

We had been looking for a building to rent for our business, in the case that we were to have one. We found one that would have to suffice, but wasn't ideal. Our former employer had negotiated with someone to build a warehouse across the street from his plant. They were running out of space and were going to rent the building for more. The company had closed down by the time the building was finished. They left the owner with a big empty warehouse that had never been used.

Joey was out of town, and I was restless, so I contacted the owner. I had met Jerry before. I looked him up in the phone book, and he was more than willing to talk to me. He was a very kind man, and he was interested in our plans. When Joey came home, we met Jerry at the building. He agreed to rent it to us at a reasonable price, but there were no offices. That presented another obstacle. But at least we had some encouragement.

Joey and I went before the board of the Small Business Administration, and they approved a loan for us, contingent on finding a bank. Finally, we were notified that a bank had agreed. It was the last one we had gone to. We couldn't believe it was actually happening.

The problem of having no offices was easily solved. There was another closed business across the street from the building we were going to rent. The owner agreed to rent us the office space until we could come up with our own. We had looked at moving into modular offices and were going to be satisfied with that. Jerry wasn't. He went to work and started building us a new office building in front of the plant. He took us with him to pick out the flooring and the wallpaper. Joey even drew up the preliminary plans. He let us design our new offices.

We closed the loan and started our new business the same week that Joey received his last severance check. My new boss wished me well and paid me through the end of the month, which was two weeks after I left. The Lord was providing.

# THE REAL TRIALS BEGIN

We bought most of our office furniture from a member of our church family. He had owned his own business at one time. We also purchased integrated accounting software from him that I had never used until my last job. Coincidentally it was the same software I had just had to learn. I was fortunate to have gained enough experience to be able to teach my employees how to use it. It looked as if everything had happened for a reason. God's timing is always best. I had canceled the pending lawsuit against our former company. The Lord was giving me more than they had taken.

Our first customer was one they had transferred from our former plant to Houston. His business alone would cost them more than my fourteen weeks of pay. I remembered David telling me six years earlier that I would probably be running the business one day. He was right. Joey and I were now running a plastics business together, in the building his former company had built across the street from its own plant.

When it came time to do our tax return for the year of our unemployment, we were surprised to see that we had earned more money that year than either of us had ever earned before. That was the year we had decided to tithe.

We decided to give even more of ourselves to our church and to the Lord. Joey took on the responsibilities of helping to organize the Sunday services. It wasn't long before he was approached and asked to become a deacon. I was so proud the Sunday morning that he stood before the church and accepted his new leadership role. God had truly blessed me beyond my expectations. Someone once told me that I was lucky. I responded by saying that luck had nothing to do with it. The Lord had blessed me, and he was ready to bless them too.

Living a Christian life doesn't mean a life free of trials and tribulations. The first year of the business was very touch and go. The sales we had counted on were not quite there by the time we got started. They never are, but we had inside information. We weren't going into this blind, or were we? The customers' sales we had counted on, based on their sales from our previous employer, were coming in far short of our predictions. One customer who had consistently high sales had dropped by 75 percent by the time we started our company. That's a huge difference for a small business just getting started. We even met with him one last time before we signed our names on the dotted line of the final paperwork for the bank, signing our lives away. He was the ordained minister who had married us. He could have told us how things had changed, but he didn't.

We also received some bad advice from someone at the Small Business Administration. I had attended a class at the SBA, which was required before they would give us a loan. I was told to reduce the amount of working capital we were requesting for our loan and then open a revolving line of credit once we started. We didn't know that no bank would give us a revolving line of credit in the early stages of the business. The cost of running the business was overwhelming. I had been told how much we were admired for taking the plunge. I thought, *Don't admire me, I'm crazy.* No sane person would do what we had done. It takes money to make money, and we didn't have a lot of that.

Every week of payroll, I'd hold my breath and hope the receivables would come in on time. We had to turn to our personal savings account when they didn't. That supply was limited and ran out quickly. We had an average of thirty–five employees, and the payroll continued to grow. Our employees were former employees of the plastics company we had worked for. Our business enabled them to go back to work. We were trying to keep them at relatively the same salaries, which was difficult for a new business.

Joey dealt with the stress of keeping the plant up and running. Some days brought more bad news than good. If any major piece of equipment went out on us, we could be doomed. We were just an inch away. Very early on, we had encountered some problems with one of the molds. The customer owned the molds. We hung their mold in our machine. Raw material—resin—is then melted and injected into the mold, producing the final product. The parts we were producing were defective. The customer needed them. We ran three shifts around the clock. Joey worked for thirty hours straight on more than one occasion. He literally left for work one morning and did not come home until the next afternoon. He was desperate to solve the problem and keep our customer satisfied. He had a lot of weight on his shoulders to prove himself. He had to prove that we could do the job. He was killing himself.

One afternoon, after he had been working all night long, he and I went for a drive. He was stressed to the point of tears. Somehow I convinced him that he needed rest to be able to function properly. Not long after that problem was solved, we encountered another one. Joey and our employees were going crazy trying to solve that dilemma. As it turned out, our electric company had more volts than were necessary going into the building. Every time they plugged in a machine, it blew a circuit board. That mistake cost us a lot of time and money.

# THE CHANCE TO BAIL

Joey and I wondered what we had gotten ourselves into. The business was losing money every month. We were made an offer by some wealthy men, two brothers who had made their millions on building a successful company and selling it. They were interested in manufacturing and were willing to bail us out. They wanted 51 percent ownership interest. The remaining 49 percent was to be divided between our existing partners and us. All of the notes would remain in our name. The liability would remain ours. They would not pay us anything for the business, but they would help us out with cash flow. They would make sure the payables stayed caught up and the payroll was made. They saw an opportunity to get a company for basically nothing.

We desperately needed the cash flow, but I found the offer insulting. It is true we weren't making a profit yet, but we were almost there. Just a few more months and things could very well be looking up for us. The decision had Joey and me completely upside down. All we could do was pray. Did God want us to stand firm in our faith and believe that he would get us through the hard times? Or was God trying to save us by sending us a way out? I definitely did not want to give up. I was too proud and too much of a fighter for that. However, I didn't want my stubbornness to be the death of us. I didn't want my stubbornness to stand in the way of God's will.

I prayed that God would help us do the right thing. I knew he was with us. I could look back over the past months and see his hand at work. We lost one customer, a loss that would have destroyed us, but another one came along in the nick of time. Our new customer asked us to fax him the invoices because he wanted to show us how fast he could get us paid! Another customer was paying us a week or two early at times. These things didn't just happen in the real world. The economy was bad. We were lucky to be paid at all. We had exhausted our savings account and needed money to make payroll, and our income tax check arrived to save the day. My mother inherited some money and in turn gave my siblings and me a small portion. I received my check just in time to put it into the business.

Signing over those checks was a difficult thing for me. I had big plans for the money. My husband and I could have been debt–free and could have gotten the driveway we so desperately wanted for our house. I prayed and realized that he had provided for our needs. People were depending on us, and we couldn't let them down. It's all God's money anyway. Without him, we would have nothing. Easy come; easy go. I believed that the Lord would continue to provide.

It wasn't in my heart to give up and give our business away. However, it was so stressful that at times, I wanted to run away and hide. I had to shut my office door to keep people from seeing me cry. Not very impressive in a business world, but it did happen on occasion. Never in my life had I not paid my bills on time. There just wasn't enough money to work with. I knew that eventually the vendors would put us on hold and business would come to a halt if a miracle didn't happen soon.

My husband seemed to be leaning toward the bailout. I was disappointed but by the same token, I completely understood it. What if I convinced him to keep trying and we failed? What if we lost everything? I had no choice but to tell him I'd sign the papers if that was what he truly wanted. After all, we needed sales to grow, and that was his area of expertise, not mine. If he gave up, I knew we could not make it. We discussed the situation, and he knew how I felt. He didn't want to give the business away either.

One day I had a revelation and shared it with him. If we gave up, there would be a tremendous amount of stress removed from our lives. On the other hand, it would also remove some of our dependence on God. Maybe God wanted us to be dependent on him to get us through our situation. So we just kept pushing along. I truly had to use my experience with the corporate scene and was glad to have it. Cash flow planning and money management were a serious part of my job responsibilities. I told Joey I would somehow manage to keep us in business if he would aggressively seek more sales. I never doubted that he could do it. I believed that the experiences we had would only make us stronger. I believed that one day we would appreciate our success that much more.

# CONFRONTING THE CHALLENGES

Things were very stressful in our personal lives as well. My brother–in–law had gone into the hospital for a heart bypass surgery and never recovered. My sister was left with two adolescent boys to raise on her own. This was such a challenging time for our family. It was difficult to explain to my young son Taylor why God had taken him. He had included him in his bedtime prayers every night. We had all prayed relentlessly for his recovery. Taylor said when he got to heaven he was going to punch Jesus in the nose. (Out of the mouths of babes.) It was difficult for me to explain to my son because I was just learning it myself. His death substantiated the fact that God does not always answer our prayers the way we would like. We buried Mike on the same day that marked the first anniversary of our business.

We didn't hear from the brothers interested in our business for a while. Joey began beating the bushes looking for new customers. I managed the money the best I could. God continued to provide the payroll. I thanked him each time I was able to make another one. We continued to get involved in the church and look for ways to serve the Lord. We began counting the Sunday contributions and making the deposit for the church. That was a ministry I enjoyed. We got involved in the children's ministry as well. Church was a major part of our lives. It had never been before. The church was our family. They were there for us without fail, every time a crisis arose. They were there to share equally in our triumphs and joys.

After a few months of waiting and wondering, we got another call from the two brothers. It seemed that something had come up in regards to the business they had sold. They had been advised not to get involved with anything else for at least a year. I was relieved. I did not want to take the offer, and now it didn't have to be my decision. We probably wouldn't have been able to talk our investors into the deal anyway. The situation took care of itself. Or rather, God took care of it. How often do we waste our time worrying?

I hoped we wouldn't live to regret the outcome. Business had gotten even slower. We had to put our production workers on a three–day work week. We knew it would be difficult for our employees to take such a pay cut; but we had to do what was necessary to keep the doors open. I just knew that God would intervene any day and things would turn around. After all, we hadn't done this on our own. I would have never done it on my own. I had learned some lessons the hard way, and that was one of them.

The three–day work week only lasted about three weeks. The cost reduction wasn't big enough. We had to reduce our payroll enough to stay in business. Our customers were all experiencing low sales. One customer pulled out completely and sent their business to China. A lot of the plastics manufacturing had been moved to China. It was impossible to compete with the low labor rates. We thought we would be safe with our local customers. They would surely be too small to take their business to China. It wouldn't be cost–effective with the high freight charges they would incur.

Unfortunately for us, one of our customers, a small local business, was purchased by a Fortune 100 company. One of their first moves was to take their business to China. We were forced to have our first layoff. We reduced the number of employees from thirty–five to nine. All that were left were the office personnel, two supervisors, and two technicians. The supervisors and technicians had to operate the machines themselves. If worse came to worse, the office personnel would be operating machines as well.

It was difficult for Joey to inform everyone of the layoff. I had the unpleasant task of dealing with creditors. Our new business was definitely not turning out to be what we had expected. It hurt me greatly to have to let everyone go. I began to feel abandoned and alone. I never expected things to get so bad. For the first time, I felt like the business might not make it. In fact, I didn't see how it possibly *could* make it. Even with the payroll reduction, the overhead was more than the revenue.

All along I had been so positive. I believed that God was on our side, and we could not fail. He gave me strength and power. Suddenly I had to rethink our situation. It might not be God's will that our business would succeed. All of this came barely a month after losing my brother–in–law. I wasn't ready for another disappointment. For a brief period, I wondered why I even prayed at all. It didn't seem like the Lord was answering. Basically, I was feeling sorry for myself. But my relationship with the Lord was such that I knew he was in control. I knew that having faith in him meant that everything would be all right, even if we lost the business. I asked for his forgiveness and then asked once again for his will to be done.

The day after we informed everyone of the layoff, we received a phone call with news of possible new business. We had been producing clothes hangers for the Dollar General stores. The Wal–Mart stores were interested in our hangers. After someone in their staff did some comparison–shopping, they contacted our customer. This gave us some new hope. Not two weeks after the layoff, we were required to call six people back. Then another customer told us that we would possibly be getting nine new molds they had purchased from a company that had gone out of business. Suddenly there was a buzz in the air. Spirits were lifted, if only a little.

I reflected on my past experiences and realized that the Lord's timing had always been perfect. His timing was never early and never too late. We just had to make it one day at a time. We had to get through the slow period and survive. God's plans were bigger than us. He had a plan for each of the people who had been laid off as well. Who knows why we had to struggle so. It could have been any number of reasons that we may never know.

I felt like the Lord was testing my faith and strength. I thought it would be one of the worst times in my life if we had to close our doors. We had put everything we had into the company to keep it going. We hadn't established a line of credit with a bank because we had not been in business long enough. We had talked to the loan officer at the bank that gave us our original loan. He said we needed to be breaking even before we requested more money.

Unfortunately, we weren't. We were forced to rely on credit cards.

Consequently, we were bombarded with low– or zero–percent–interest credit card applications in the mail. It was certainly not a remedy of choice but of necessity, we thought. It was that or lose it all. Our newly acquired debt had reached six figures and was still rising. This may not seem like a lot to some people, but for the average working–class citizen, it is overwhelming. This was in excess of the initial loan we had received for the startup of the business. If the business didn't turn around and become lucrative enough to take care of this liability, we would never be able to on our own. We would have financial problems like we had never seen before. I struggled with the weight of this on my shoulders for a while. I was miserable. No one is closer to the financial problems than the chief financial officer. If it had only been so easy as to quit and walk away, but it wasn't. We were in too deep.

We just had to regroup. We had to think smarter. We had to be as lean as we could possibly be. I prayed constantly. I had to come to terms with our situation. I asked the Lord to give me strength to get through this period in my life if it was his will for the business to fail. I tried to accept that it might fail. I tried to accept that it might be his will. What a relief to turn it over to him, to put it in his hands. I knew he would be with us whatever the outcome. At that moment, we were exactly where we were supposed to be. These are things I had to keep telling myself.

Sadly enough, the situation just kept getting worse. It actually came to a point where we had no idea what would happen next. We had no money to pay for raw materials. Without raw materials, we could not make any products. Things looked more hopeless than ever. Our customer turned down the Wal-Mart business, and we didn't get any of the nine molds from the other. Even Jack, our materials manager and friend, had started to show his concern. Jack had always been optimistic. I often looked to him for words of encouragement. Joey, Jack, and I had spent a lot of time together discussing the business over lunch. Jack had become worried. He told me that there came a time to face reality. It seemed very doubtful that the business would turn around.

Much to my despair, Joey sent out a résumé. He heard of an opening with a local company and applied for the job. I wasn't surprised that he got an interview. I didn't like anything about the situation. Joey was trying to use preventive maintenance. He was worried about us both losing our jobs again and having no income. But I felt like he was giving up on our business and giving in. I knew I had to let Joey make his own decision, so I didn't say much about it. Instead, I prayed. I wasn't ready to give up. I thought him being somewhere else would ensure the demise of our company. I decided that I would do my best to run the business without him.

*Stubborn* is probably a good word to describe me, or *determined*. I put it in God's hands and didn't worry about it. Joey's interview lasted several hours. When he returned, I asked him how it went. The position was for shift work. He would not be able to go to church with the boys and me very often. He would have to give up his responsibilities at the church. He didn't want to do that. I knew he would not do that. My prayers had been answered. I was relieved.

It seemed to me that someone had tried a few times to give us a way out. It's hard to determine whether the Lord is testing your faith or throwing you a lifeline. Maybe the devil himself was interfering. Selling our business for nothing or walking away from it all and taking another job were two of the choices we had been given. Either one would take away our dependence on God. The latter would even take away some of Joey's work for him. We would take our chances and keep trudging along.

# SEARCHING FOR ANSWERS

We looked to our investors for help. Joey and I had given all we had in cash and had used all the available credit we had. Our initial risk in the business was very small compared to what it ended up being. Our investors were not willing to help. After all, we had lost $350,000 during the first full year. Who could blame them? They decided they would rather cut their losses with their original investment. That was disappointing to Joey and me. We didn't feel we had that luxury. Again, we were in too deep. It had to be all or nothing. The business meant too much for us to walk away. I had decided I would be there until we were forced to close the doors. I could not make the decision to give up, even if things seemed hopeless. Things definitely seemed hopeless. I always told myself that it wasn't over until it was over. I was not a quitter.

The time finally came when we had outstanding invoices that we could not pay. There were no more credit cards. After receiving a plethora of them, they finally quit coming. I could not believe the number of cards and amount of credit we were able to get.

We could have paid for our house and SUV with the amount we had charged! We were going to be shut down. For at least two days, Joey and I thought that it was over. I was heartsick once again. I couldn't help but feel like the Lord had let me down. I guessed the message I'd heard that day about taking risks wasn't meant for me. I felt like Peter walking on the water. The Lord told me to step out of the boat, and I jumped in. I did not expect the business to fail. I did not expect to lose everything. I felt like the Lord had promised me it would work if I were willing to take the risk. I had to do a lot of soul–searching. I was in constant conversation with God. I had spent the past year reading the Bible in my office in my spare time. I had read it completely through once and had started over again.

I pulled my strength from the Scriptures and what I knew to be true from my past experiences. The verses that talked of Peter walking on water actually read:

> Then Peter got down out of the boat, walked on the water and came toward Jesus. But when he saw the wind, he was afraid and, beginning to sink, cried out, "Lord save me!" Immediately Jesus reached out his hand and caught him. "You of little faith," he said, "why did you doubt?"
>
> Mathew 14:29–31

God had a plan for us. God's timing was perfect. We did not have to be afraid because we had encountered a storm. I knew that the reason it was okay to take the risk was because, win or lose, we would be fine. That was God's promise. I prayed that he would save our business if it was his will. I prayed that he would give me strength to accept his will if it wasn't. It reminded me of Jesus praying on the Mount of Olives before his crucifixion. "Father, if you are willing, take this cup from me; yet not my will, but yours be done" (Luke 22:42).

After two days of hopelessness, our customer offered to pay for the materials and deduct it from his payment to us. He wanted to help us keep going. However, in good faith, we had to pay the vendor the oldest invoice of seven thousand dollars. We didn't have seven thousand dollars, and we didn't have any idea where to get it.

That night I went home and played back my messages on the phone. There was a message from a financial institution saying that our loan had been approved and we could come pick up the money. I thought it was a joke. We hadn't applied for a loan. Then I remembered that I reluctantly had mailed in one final application for credit that we had received in the mail. Several weeks prior I had sent it off with no hope of being approved. The amount was $7,500.00. On the way to pick up the money, we turned on the radio in the truck and heard the same message I had heard almost two years before. The preacher was talking about taking risks and trusting in God.

That same week, we had to come up with another seven thousand dollars for a different customer's materials. My mother gave us a check for eight thousand dollars that she had on credit. We were in business another week. It was truly a day–to–day thing. We had no idea where the next dollar would come from. We were losing money every month. There was no possible way for things to get better unless we got more business.

We knew we needed to cut costs more, but there wasn't much more to be cut. I had reduced our salaries and the other ones that would make a difference would be the supervisors'. We didn't know what to do. We knew that we would need the supervisors if business picked up. If we laid them off, we would probably lose them for good. One day our quality manager hurt his leg while loading a truck. He would miss months of work and be paid by our insurance company. Because he had some other health issues, he ended up taking an extended leave of absence. Thus, we were forced to learn to do without him, and we received a little relief from payroll. However, our insurance went up. When our first shift supervisor turned in his notice, I didn't blink. I thought that the Lord must be doing what we needed but didn't have the nerve to do on our own. However, before his notice was up, he canceled his request. Something happened, and he did not get the job he thought he was taking.

During the midst of all of our troubles, we had some friends lose their business. Bill and Dona went to our church. They had owned their own business. This was difficult for me also. It's almost like being pregnant and your close friend having a miscarriage. It brings the horrible possibilities very close to home. We prayed for them. We reached out to them. We were people who could understand what they were going through.

One day we met for lunch. During the conversation, it was mentioned that we were in desperate need of a good salesperson. It wasn't working out for Joey to have that responsibility. It needed to be a full–time priority. Joey wasn't able to devote all of his time to sales. Bill had a lot of sales experience, so we invited him to our plant to look around. We explained to him that we didn't have the money to pay for a full–time employee. We were hoping to pay on a commission basis. He agreed to try to sell for us. That stirred up a little hope again. However, Bill needed money immediately. He took a job traveling out of town and informed us that he would try to help us out on his days off.

For a brief moment, I thought I could see God's plan. That must be it. He must have intended for Bill to save our business and help himself at the same time. Two Christian families in desperate need could come together and solve the problems for each. It seems I analyzed things too much. I didn't know what God's plan was. He would reveal it to me in his own time. In the meantime, we had to learn to live with our situation. It was a way of life, whether we liked it or not.

An important but hard lesson to learn is that being Christians does not give us a guarantee of success. Jesus suffered. We all have to suffer. Although I obviously had my doubts at times, I had such a strong feeling that God had called us to take on this business. Joey and I both wrestled with our emotions. We prayed for peace, and we did get peace. It was a struggle, but I believe we both came to a place where we could finally let go. We were not leaving. God would either save us, or we would be forced to leave. Once again, we looked back at all the happenings over the past year and a half. We knew God had been with us all the way. He had saved us time and time again. I kept hearing the message, "Don't give up."

The cash flow and credit situation had gotten so bad that I was actually relieved! I knew that it meant that the time was coming soon for some relief. It got interesting. I would go to work and ask God, "What are you going to do to get us through this one?" I didn't have a clue, but I knew it would be interesting to watch.

The new year was coming, which meant I had twelve thousand dollars of property taxes due. I had quarterly taxes for payroll due as well. With no money even to pay for raw materials, where would we get the money for the taxes? As soon as January arrived, I rushed my financial information to the CPAs and had my tax return done. I was embarrassed to show them our income statement. I knew that they, as well as our bankers, had to be wondering how we were still hanging on. I'm sure they thought we would be gone very quickly. The good news was that we were due a refund of more than fifteen thousand dollars. Joey and I were getting back everything we had paid in because of the business loss. I borrowed money from my mother against the refund in order to pay the taxes on time. We made it through another January.

February came and brought better news. Four potential customers Joey had called on many times before had decided they were interested in moving their business to us. Joey suddenly had many new parts to quote. We had to take it in stride, though. We had high hopes before and nothing happened. The difference was that I knew we were at a turning point. I knew this would make or break us and, knowing God's timing, I believed help was on its way.

Joey and I were ready for a break. We had signed up to take a cruise with some church friends almost a year in advance. The time had finally arrived to go. We were worried about the timing but would lose our money if we didn't take the trip. We had gotten a good group rate. I prayed that we would have some good news before we left so that we could enjoy our trip and maybe even celebrate. We got a call on the Thursday before we left from one of the customers informing us that we would begin to get some of their business within a week. That next Monday we were on our way to Galveston. We had gotten the good news we were praying for. We were thankful that our supervisor had not left. He must have been part of the plan.

We took our much–needed vacation and escaped reality for a little while. It was during that trip that I had another realization. Spending that time with our church family and realizing how much we loved them made me realize how blessed we were. It could have been easy to overlook the blessings. So many times it seemed as if we could not possibly make it another day. Our happiness and well–being didn't depend on the success of our business. We were blessed abundantly with our children, our family, and our friends. We had some friends whose daughter was sick. She needed a kidney transplant and was on a waiting list to receive one. We had some more friends whose daughter had leukemia. I could always think of worse things than what we were going through. I had a lot to be thankful for, and I was.

# SURVIVING ON MIRACLES

When we came home from our cruise, things were a little more optimistic. We were still getting by one day at a time. It's amazing how long that went on. We got a little new business but not enough to make us break even. I had thought we were at a breaking point, but we continued to struggle along in the same manner for a couple more months.

I wonder if other people truly get to see God's hands in their business. Looking back, it actually makes me thankful for the experience. Our God is an awesome God! It was remarkable how many times I would need more money to pay the rent or the electric bill and someone would unexpectedly send a check in the mail before it was due. I remember praying on the way to the post office and how extremely grateful I would be to find a check in the box. I would make payroll with fifteen dollars to spare. I would be holding a payment in my drawer that needed to go out and return to work the next day to find a check on my desk. We had sold some pallets to a business in the area. The money was just enough to cover my payment. God was providing. There was no room for comfort, but he was providing.

Joey and I both grew tired of our situation. You never know the answers, even when you think you do. We would come to rely on God saving us from each problem that would arise so much that we would begin to second–guess him. We would be wrong. I got busy and threw myself into trying to find a way to come up with some additional working capital. I contacted the office of our member of the Texas House of Representatives. We had meetings with the Texas Agriculture Rural Department, a lady from the governor's office, the local economic development people, and several others. We were trying to get information or knowledge that could be beneficial to us in our situation. I was hoping to get information on available grants or loans to small businesses. I did discover one such grant that had to be accompanied by a loan. We had to find a bank willing to do us a favor.

We met with a local bank hoping to appeal to his desire of keeping businesses in the community. I knew we didn't have much of a chance of getting the loan. We had completely overextended ourselves in unsecured debt. All of our collateral was tied up with the bank that had given us our original loan. I anxiously waited a week for the results. I did have a little hope knowing that God could accomplish things we could not. Nevertheless, I wasn't very surprised to hear that they would not help us. I thought that God must have another plan for us. Something else would happen around the corner, because we had once again come to a point of desperately needing money to continue.

Our local economic development center was concerned and expressed a strong willingness to help. They hired a consultant from the Texas Manufacturing Assistance Center to do an assessment of our business. This would help us to see things that maybe we had not seen. It would help us become more efficient and more productive. The person who came to do the job gave me a contact name for a Tyler bank that was known to lend money to manufacturers.

I called the man, and he faxed me an application for a fifty–thousand–dollar, unsecured loan. The application had to be signed by our partners as well as us. It just so happened that our partners had contacted us two days before and suggested we meet. We hadn't met with them in a long time. We were under the impression that they were not willing to help. They came into the office right after I received the fax. We explained our needs to them and they took home a copy of the papers to be signed. The next day, they faxed me the signed copy of the application.

Joey and I both felt strongly that we would get the loan. Everything had fallen into place perfectly.

I was quite disappointed when the loan officer called me and said he would not be able to be of assistance. Apparently that wasn't the plan around the corner. Once again, we knew just enough to know we did not know anything. We knew we had to keep looking to God. Only he had the answers that would one day be revealed to us.

I notified our partners that the loan fell through. The next day Connie contacted me and told me she had taken out a personal loan through her place of employment. The money would be wired to our account in the next day or two. That's how long the money lasted, about two days. We were temporarily saved, again. We continuously struggled and wrestled with so many thoughts going through our minds. Joey and I went to lunch together that day, and the conversation was all too familiar. Were we acquiring more and more debt never to be paid back if the business failed? Or were we buying the business enough time to grow and become profitable in the end? The conclusion we always came to was that we would not be the ones to give up. If we gave up, we were giving up on God. If the doors remained open, there was always a chance of recovery. Once they closed, it was over forever. We figured God would continue to save us and eventually turn things around, or the business would eventually, sooner rather than later, shut down. We were leaving the door open for God to work. I couldn't help but wonder how long we would have to live in limbo. It was torture to live that way. Even with the peace that comes along with faith, it was a great struggle to overcome our fears.

Managing the business was a great test of our abilities. We now had so many credit card payments to make, the debt was enormous. Somehow I had been managing to make all of the payments on time. I did not want to ruin our credit. The problem was that we had too much credit. The banks began to send us letters stating they were increasing our annual percentage rates to outrageous amounts. I responded with letters rejecting the terms and closing the accounts. We had already used most of the available credit anyway. I kept a spreadsheet on all of the cards. Juggling statements from all of those cards was not fun. Several times we were charged fees for late payments and received rate increases that were not justified. I had to call and have them removed. On two different occasions we had purchases made to our cards that were not legitimate. Someone had acquired our account numbers and used them illegally. The credit card ordeal was definitely a test of my organization skills. Again, it certainly wasn't a method of choice but necessity, we thought. It kept our doors open.

# TESTING OUR ENDURANCE

Slowly, gradually, the business started to come in. We gained one new customer in March. In May we added two more. Things were finally moving in the right direction. We still had a huge problem with cash flow. We needed money to buy the raw materials for the new business. There were no more credit cards. I went to our original lender one more time. I asked them to revisit our situation and see if there was any way they could help us out. That time it was a little different. We had still not reached the break–even point, but we could see it in the near future, if we had the bank's help. Basically, they had to decide to give us another loan, or let us close our doors with the new business already in house. Our loan officer told us that our chances were "very slim." We gave him a long list of action items that we were taking in order to improve our company, along with fore-casted sales for the next two years, and much more information he requested. Then once again, we had to wait.

The lack of a full–time salesperson was still one of our biggest problems. We still could not afford one. It needed to be, and was, one of the key matters on our action items. It obviously wasn't working for Joey. He didn't have the necessary time to dedicate to finding new business. I had more time on my hands than he did. The manufacturing representatives we had were not bringing enough to the table.

I had absolutely no experience in sales, which I guess is the reason it took me so long to make the effort. It took me a long time to realize where to start. It really was quite simple. I used the Internet. I used the chamber of commerce Web sites for surrounding areas. We had brochures printed with our company information. I typed a cover letter and mailed them out to business after business. We needed to get our name out there. We were two months shy of being in business two years, and we were finally getting some advertisement. We obviously could not depend on the business we thought we had. I mailed the first batch of letters on a Wednesday. On Thursday we received a call from one of the companies that had gotten our information. We were given several parts to quote on. That was a great incentive for me to keep going.

Our loan officer, Troy, told us that he was submitting our request to his corporate officers on Thursday of the next week. We had to manage to survive until then. Friday came and we talked to him. The answer wasn't no, but it wasn't yes either. They were very hesitant, but they requested more information. In the meantime, he had learned of a new loan program through the East Texas Council of Government. They had given us part of our original loan as well as the bank. We had asked for $100,000 from the bank. The ETCOG loan could have been up to $185,000. That started the wheels turning in my head again. Maybe God didn't give us the loan from the bank so that we could get the loan from ETCOG and get *more* money.

I spoke to Luke at ETCOG, and he told me where to pull the application from the Internet. I filled out the paperwork and sent it in that same day. They would not be able to meet for two more weeks. We were in desperate need of cash, and the loans kept getting pushed back. When the next payroll came around, we didn't have it. We had always managed to come up with it, but that time we didn't have any of it. My mother bailed us out once again. The ETCOG board was meeting the next day, so the plan was to pay her back immediately. Joey and I both felt very good about the loan. We felt strongly that we would get it. He met with the board and answered their questions. They sent him off with a request for more information. It would be another week before they could meet and discuss it again.

Meanwhile we tried to maintain our composure. As I said before, it was a way of life. If we responded with chaos every time we had a setback, we would be living in constant chaos. It was a real test of our endurance. Finally they met again. Joey went before the board once more then left the room so they could make their decision. I spoke to him on the phone while he waited. He told me that things had gone well, and he would be surprised if we didn't get it. They called him back in and politely told him they declined to make the loan. He called me on his way to the office and gave me the news. We were both very disappointed. That same week, we were notified by one of our customers that they were pulling their mold. They had been quoted a cheaper price from someone else, and we couldn't match it. It seemed like we were continuously getting the wind knocked out of our sails. As the old saying goes, one step forward and two steps back. I didn't get the money to repay my mother.

I made it through the rest of the day and almost the rest of the weekend. Sunday came and we were sitting in church. The sermon was on Romans 8:28, "And we know that in all things God works for the good of those who love him, who have been called according to his purpose." I fought back the tears through most of the service and finally ducked into an empty room to escape the crowd.

The room wasn't empty. A close friend of mine happened to be in there with her newborn child. She knew about our situation and greeted me with a hug. We talked for a little bit, and I cried. I wanted to keep crying and crying, but I couldn't. I had to dry my eyes and round up my children and get them to class. On the way to lunch, I just wanted to go home. It was my parents' anniversary, and we were going to eat with them. How I wanted to be at home lying in my bed. The only time I wasn't feeling the pain was when I was asleep.

# LEARNING TO BE STILL

It was the end of June. July would mark two years that we had been struggling with our business. I knew God was there. I knew things would work out according to his will. I was just tired, so tired. I would pray and look up to heaven and imagine God's hand literally coming out of the clouds and taking hold of me. I wanted to be where God wanted me to be, wherever that was.

The thing that weighed the heaviest on my mind had to do with my mother. My mother and father had always struggled to make ends meet. They were always helping other people, no matter if they had to do without. I remember my mother skipping meals so that her children had enough to eat. My father had many health–related problems over the years and missed a lot of work. I had always been so independent and determined to make it on my own. I was not going to be one of the ones to take from them. One of my greatest reasons for wanting our own business was so that I could make life easier for my mother. I wanted to give her a place to retire comfortably. I wanted to be able to pay her well and give her some of the perks she had never had before. The tables were turned. She inherited some money when her mother passed away. She came to our rescue several times when things seemed hopeless. The thought of not being able to repay her devastated me.

In a strange way, I came to feel like that was part of the plan. I remember at different times in my life making comments to my mom that were probably hurtful to her. When she would be there to give someone money to help them pay their rent or buy them groceries, I had made remarks about how I had to make it on my own. I had gone through some difficult times in my life when I felt alone because I didn't see it as an option to take from my parents. Maybe my mom felt like she was never able to help me because I never asked for it or never needed it.

She worked with me on a daily basis. She saw what we were going through. When she knew we were in trouble, she gave without hesitation. She gave without expectation of being paid back. I know she was glad to be able to help. Maybe, as a mother, she needed that. As a daughter, though, I needed to repay her. How ironic it would be for me to be the one who took some of her inheritance and lost it. I could handle being broke; I had been broke before. What I couldn't handle was losing other people's money—my mother's or our investors'.

Joey and I prayed fervently and took comfort in knowing that God was in control. I strongly believed that it was God's will that we had been turned down so many times. If he had wanted any of the loans to go through, they would have. We still had one last chance. The bank still had us on the back burner. We spoke to Troy and told him we were turned down by ETCOG. He had another meeting the following week with his board. He came to our office and met with us to discuss more information that might be helpful in getting the loan approved. I created charts and graphs and updated forecasts and sent them to him for his meeting. We had talked about another scenario when we met. We were going to ask ETCOG to revisit the situation and see if they would pay a reduced amount to be matched by the bank. If Troy could tell his board members that ETCOG was willing to do that, it would increase his chances of getting the loan. We spoke to Luke the same morning that Troy was to meet with his people. He told us that they agreed to consider our request. That same morning, we received two unexpected phone calls. Two different companies we had dealt with during our previous employment called to tell us they wanted to give us their business. They were unhappy with their suppliers and wanted to change. We called Troy to inform him of ETCOG's decision and to inform him that we had just gained two more new customers. Then the ball was in his court.

So once again we waited. We waited for the phone call from Troy to tell us the bank's final decision. Of course it didn't come that day. The next morning I went to town instead of going directly to work. I had some shopping to do, and I couldn't stand the waiting. I drove by our church on the way to the office and read the sign out front. "God never gets in a hurry, but he is always on time." That couldn't have been truer. I had seen it over and over again in my life, and definitely in our business.

The call didn't come until a week later. Another weekend went by for us to ponder everything. The whole situation was so frustrating. Finally Troy called and gave us good news. The bank decided to give us a loan with the condition that ETCOG would match their amount as we had discussed. We were very relieved and grateful. Luke had told us that he felt confident going into their meeting. We spent the day with lifted spirits and feeling as if everything would be okay.

Then we got a call from Luke. He sounded down when I said hello. I thought he was playing with me. (Luke was also a friend of ours and member of our church at one time.) He wasn't joking. He dreaded to tell me the bad news. ETCOG turned us down once again. Once again, we were surprised and confused.

Once again we felt let down. We had almost taken for granted that we were on our way to better days. We were back to square one. How long would God continue to let us wonder where he wanted us to be? If our business wasn't part of our purpose, what was? We were closer to losing everything than ever before.

We had actually spent the entire day thinking our struggle had finally ended. It seemed so cruel. We had been praying for God to show us a sign that our business was going to survive. We had gained five new customers. It seemed like mixed messages. We had no money to purchase materials to make the new customers' products. Were we going to have to turn them away? It was so hard not to feel angry. I wanted to make sense of it all, but I couldn't.

I had to pull myself together, pick up my children, and go home. They were so innocent. They didn't have a clue what we were dealing with. It was very difficult for me to function. I was so tired. My soon–to–be–three–year–old was still fighting sleep at eleven that night. I held him in my arms and rocked him and prayed. That was how it all began. More than two years before, I'd sat in my chair late at night, nursed my son, and prayed. I prayed ceaselessly that we would make the right decision about whether to start our business. I prayed incessantly that God wouldn't let it happen if it were only our will and not his. I prayed that he would not let it happen if we were going to lose our investors' money. Where did I go wrong? Joey and I both knew that we had not gone into this without God. I wished I knew what God had in mind. I wished I knew what the outcome would be.

I was so tired of squirming. "Be still, and know that I am God" (Psalm 46:10). I believed I had figured out what that verse meant. It was very difficult to be still. I absolutely did not want to return to work the next day. Vendors were calling, and I did not know how or when I would be able to pay them.

I never imagined that I would dread going to work at my own business. On one hand, it was wonderful. I loved my job. I loved the flexibility and being able to spend time with my children. On the other hand, the stress of making payroll and paying the bills was tremendous. I was uneasy every time the phone rang.

However, I had to go to work that day. My mother had jury duty, and Joey had to make a business trip to Houston. I could not leave Jack to handle the phones and do everything by himself. As usual I was forced to face the issue instead of running away. I went to work and dealt with my responsibilities. I did have to speak to some vendors wanting payments. That made me so uncomfortable. I hated that part of the job. I wished someone could fire me, because I couldn't quit. Some of our vendors were very understanding and easy to talk to. We were making partial payments to some when we could. Others were disgruntled. I understood why. I knew we owed the money. We had taken the goods, and we owed the money. I just didn't have it. No matter how much of a lecture I received, the outcome was the same. I paid what I could.

I had been telling the vendors that we were in the process of getting working capital for the business. Every time things were delayed, we had to explain it to them somehow. There were a lot of apologies being made. Unless we were to give up and go home, something still had to be done. I contemplated our dilemma and tried to figure out my next move. I decided that we still had one minute chance left. It was a far stretch, but I didn't have an alternate plan.

I contacted the local economic development company and asked them to consider matching the seventy–five–thousand–dollar amount Regions Bank had agreed to lend. I explained the recent events that had taken place and was told they would bring it up at their next meeting. I couldn't believe we were waiting again. I was upset when the last opportunity fell through with ETCOG, but it wasn't because I thought there was no hope left. It was because I was ready for the battle to end. I have always hated roller coasters. I was tired of the ride. I wanted it to stop and let me off. I knew God could come in at the very last minute and turn things all around. I kept reminding myself of the saying I'd read on the sign at church. "God is never in a hurry, but he is always on time." It's just that when we think we can't take any more, it goes on a little longer. The board would not be able to meet again for another two weeks; two more weeks of explaining, apologizing, and negotiating to get raw materials.

When the day arrived that the board would meet, I was anxious, to say the least. I felt like crawling out of my skin to be more exact. I had tears in my eyes on the way to work, far before the meeting began. The buildup of pressure and anxiety was getting to me. I needed to explode. I felt like I was bracing for the hard punch I was about to receive to my stomach. This time I felt like it was our last chance. I had no idea where to turn if this fell through.

Several times before, I had felt fairly confident and had been disappointed. This time, I didn't know what to think. Joey had said that we would start looking for a buyer to purchase the business if we didn't get the loan. They would be determining our future in that board meeting. I knew it was in God's hands once again. They couldn't do anything that he would not allow. It might be his will for us to move on. We were ready to accept his will. That didn't mean that I would not be temporarily devastated. It would be very painful for me to admit failure and lose all the money that was invested, especially my mother's.

I read another message on a church sign one day that said, "People do not fail, they give up." We had not given up. There was some comfort in that. But I knew I would feel like we had failed. It would be very humbling. I e-mailed several of our close friends and asked them to say a prayer for us that day. By the end of the day, I would either be ecstatic or miserable.

At five o'clock, the two gentlemen from Gedco arrived at our office. The first one smiled and hugged me. The second one said, "It's bad news." The board had said no, three to zero. I couldn't get past the, "It's bad news." I heard it echoing over and over in my head. We thanked them for their efforts and they left. It was then time to rush off to Tyler and eat supper with a supplier we had planned to meet. I still had no time for exploding. I was miserable inside but had to smile through our meal. We didn't want to discuss with our dinner companion what had happened. The forty-five minute drive to and from Tyler gave Joey and me time to talk. We both felt so disappointed and let down yet again. We had no idea where to turn next. We felt like we had lost everything.

I cried and prayed myself to sleep again that night. I woke up the next day with a better outlook. That's the way I handled things. Bad news hit me like a ton of bricks. It knocked me down, but I got back up. I asked Joey to put off trying to find a buyer for a little while longer. I had no plan; I just wasn't ready yet. I prayed that God would let me know if it was time to give up. It certainly looked like it. But it still didn't feel like it. I told God that he would have to show me where to go and what to do next. I had exhausted all of my resources. If help were to come, he would have to send it to us. "Be still, and know that I am God" (Psalm 46:10). Be still and let God.

# GOD IS IN CONTROL

That Sunday night, Joey had been asked to give a lesson at church. They had been asking different members to give "straight from the heart" talks. He stood in front of the congregation and talked about what his favorite verse meant to him. Romans 8:28, "And we know that in all things God works for the good of those who love him, who have been called according to his purpose." He talked about God's timing in our lives. He talked about our situation with our business and how we had been totally dependent on God. He told everyone that we had received bad news that week and that our business was in serious jeopardy.

I sat and listened with my head down, wiping away the tears. When church was over, we had an overwhelming response from our church family. People were touched by what he had said. They cared about what we were going through. Several people asked us about our problem and were very concerned. That lit a tiny spark of hope in my heart again. We could feel the power of their prayers.

We went back to work the next Monday not knowing what would happen. The only thing we could think of was to ask the bank to defer our note payments for a few months. That would give us forty–five hundred dollars a month to pay for materials. We asked the question and then had to wait for the answer. We were running out of material quickly. The bank didn't give us an answer for several days. Finally, on the last possible day we could order more materials to keep us from stopping production, the bank agreed to defer our payment for three months. We placed an order for next–day delivery and were in business for a little while longer. The next week we gained another new customer. The sales for our recently acquired customers were continuing to rise. Things were looking a little brighter. It seemed like God was answering my prayers, telling me it wasn't time to quit. We still had no money to spare, not even enough to pay the bills, but we were still in business. When we can see no sunlight through the clouds, God can.

So many times we thought it was over. We thought we were going to shut down. We thought if we didn't get a loan, we couldn't make it. But each time we were turned down, we managed to keep going a little longer. Days would go by, and before we knew it, days turned into weeks. Strange as it seems, I felt more at peace. God showed us that we didn't have to have the loan to make it. He continued to provide what we needed. Over and over again he showed us he would provide. It finally got through. I began to feel like we would make it with or without the help from the bank.

More than a month had gone by since Gedco had turned us down. Cash flow was getting better, ever so slightly. We still had large amounts of money owed to vendors that we couldn't pay. I was still making partial payments when I could. It would be a long time before we could pay them off in full. The vendors weren't happy with us. Our main supplier would release more material only after we made a payment on our account. One of our customers had another tool transferred to us, and with it came material; material that we could use for our other products as well as theirs. Jack told me that we wouldn't have made it without that material. I told him it was part of God's plan to keep us going. I never thought of the unexpected as coincidences. It was God at work.

I had all but given up on getting any more working capital, but I hated owing people money that I couldn't pay. I was looking over some old loan information I still had lying around in my office. I had looked at it all before, but I decided to revisit some sites on the Internet. There was a fund I had read about but ruled out some time before. It wasn't near enough for what we needed. For some reason, I decided to inquire about it anyway.

I placed a call to the governor's office and left a message for someone to return my call. I hadn't given it much thought, but after a few days someone did return my call. This person told me what I already knew about the fund. It had a maximum amount of thirty–five thousand dollars. However, she gave me a phone number for someone else who might be able to help. She said they would be more likely to help than a traditional lender. It was called the Texas Mezzanine Fund. I made the call. I explained our situation of needing someone to match our bank's seventy–five–thousand–dollar commitment. I explained that our financial history was very lacking but things were improving. As did everyone, they requested piles of information be faxed to them along with the application. I went through all the motions. I didn't have anything to lose. It no longer seemed like life or death. Everything wasn't depending on it going through. Again, I just prayed that God's will would be done. We had been taking things much too seriously in the past.

It's so much easier to handle situations when you realize that God is in control. We knew that and believed that all along. But you have to accept it with everything inside you. It's just so difficult. You have to understand that you didn't get that loan because

God didn't want you to. It makes no sense to hold a grudge. Each person who turned us away was just another tool being used to accomplish God's plan. You just move on and pray that he points you in the right direction. We were ready to go wherever he would lead us. God is sovereign over even death. That means there is no situation too impossible for him to overcome.

I felt like I was finally getting a grip on things. We didn't have the money for the next payroll, but I knew inside that it would come. I just knew. However, it wasn't until five o'clock on Thursday, payday being Friday morning, that we were informed we would get a check from a customer. There's nothing like living on the edge. How could a person continue in that situation without God's peace?

I had been dealing with a lady from the Texas Mezzanine Fund for several weeks. One day we spoke, and she told me that she had been given the green light on our loan. She was going to talk to our bank about releasing some collateral, but she didn't think that would make or break the deal. I was greatly encouraged by our conversation. I actually thought that the quest had finally come to an end. We thought we had nowhere else to turn when the last one fell through. Suddenly we found ourselves about to get the money we so desperately needed.

The final meeting was on a Monday, and no one had called by Thursday. When I could wait no longer, I called and left a message for Theresa to return my call. I was closing up my office for the day and running the computer backups after five o'clock when the phone rang. It was Theresa. Very nonchalantly she told me that she had no luck with our request. We talked several minutes before what she said finally sank in. We were turned down again. She apologized for being misleading. She explained that she did her best but was sometimes wrong. There was no way she could know her role in our ongoing endeavors. I could do nothing but thank her for her time and effort. It was just another day's work for her, another phone call.

It became ever so clear to me that there was *no one* who was going to lend us money. Our bank held all of the collateral for our original loan. They could afford to give us additional funds and still be in good standing. I went to Troy, our loan officer, for what seemed like the one–hundredth final time. One of our vendors had now turned us over to a collection agency. I had somehow prevented that for over two years. I needed the money to bring us back to a level playing field. We had two new customers who had placed over sixty thousand dollars in purchase orders due within one month's time. I faxed the purchase orders to Troy in an effort to show him that our forecasted sales were substantiated. That dollar volume would finally allow us to exceed our break–even point. The company had a realistic chance of becoming self–sufficient and viable. It was all right within our grasp. If we could not purchase the raw materials, we could not make the product, and therefore would lose the customer we had worked so hard to get.

Troy promised to promote our cause to his committee once again. I wished that I could promote our cause to his superiors. I somehow didn't feel that he would be as passionate in pleading our case as I would have been. But that wasn't an option. I had no choice but to trust him and do what we had been trained so well to do: wait.

This time I told him that we needed him to expedite the process. We had waited and waited and there was no more time to waste. He kept in touch with me, and after the first week, he gave me good news. His boss had reviewed everything and had approved our request. Surely, this time was it. We were finally going to get the working capital. All he had to do was run it by one more person, the top guy in charge. Meanwhile I'm telling vendors that they would hopefully be getting their money soon. It looked like the loan was going to go through.

A few days later Troy called us back and ever so politely told us it didn't happen. Oh well, this wasn't the first time we had been given high hopes only to be disappointed. Even with all of the purchase orders that were due in November, his higher–up didn't think we had a chance. They were sitting pretty if we went under, and he wanted to keep it that way.

God continued to answer our prayers. We didn't get any outside help as far as a loan goes, but somehow we managed to keep getting raw materials. A major factor in that happening was help we received from a friend, a person we had dealt with and gotten to know during our previous employment. He worked for a resin supplier. He convinced his people to work out a deal with us. They would ship material to our plant and bill us on consignment. We would inform them when we had used so many pounds, and they would send us an invoice. This bought us more time before we had to come up with the money. For people who seemed to have no luck at all, we were actually pretty lucky. It obviously wasn't God's plan for us to get a loan, but it didn't seem to be his plan for us to close down either.

# SEARCHING FOR THE CROSS

We made it through the month. November 2004 was our best month. We finally showed a profit. After two and a half years, we finally had a positive bottom line. What a great feeling that was! I had longed for the day that I did the financial statements and saw a positive number. That, by no means, meant that we were out of the woods. We had two and a half years of debt to pay back. We owed our vendors lots of money. We needed things that we were having great difficulty getting. We still desperately needed money.

I contacted our friend at East Texas Regional Development again. I told him the bank had turned us down once again. I told him we finally had good numbers to show. I sent him our November financial statements, and he took them to his board meeting that week. The board discussed it and gave us a pat on the back. They were glad to see that things were improving; however, they wanted to see another month or so of this improvement before they would reconsider giving us more money. The way the system works is that no one will give you money until you can prove you don't need it.

We were heading into the holidays. It seemed we could see a tiny speck of light peeking through at the end of the very long tunnel. Then we got a phone call from our latest new customer; the one whose sales had thrown us over the break–even point. We had made hundreds of plastic mouse pads and shipped them by boat to Germany. The parts were perfect when they left our plant. When they arrived in Germany a couple of weeks later, they were warped. I thought, *Are you kidding me?* Was this some kind of joke? Could life be any more cruel?

This company owed us twenty–five thousand dollars that we needed badly. We had no idea what the repercussions of it all would be. Should I even say that we were disappointed? Joey ended up having several conversations with our customer. We had made the parts according to specifications we had received from him. He himself had approved the parts before they were shipped. We had no way of knowing what would happen. He apparently agreed. He agreed to pay us the money he owed then pay half of the cost to reproduce the product. We couldn't be sure until we had the money in hand. It would remain to be seen.

We had a four–day weekend for the Christmas holiday. Joey was obviously feeling down. He definitely did not have the Christmas spirit. I didn't either. We never quit believing in God, but it still was no fun going through all of the ups and downs. I got on my knees alone in my room that night and prayed. I asked a special prayer for strength for my husband. I asked God to give him the extra help he needed to lift his spirits and let him enjoy Christmas. I had no idea how that would happen.

We were home for the weekend. I didn't expect any news from our business. For some reason, Joey decided to run to the office. He was only there for a brief time, but he noticed there was a message on the answering machine. He played the message. He had been quoting on a job for a potential customer. That customer left a message saying that the project was a go. We would be getting a hundred–thousand–dollar project in the next couple of months. When Joey came back home, he was renewed. I found it odd that someone would call and leave that kind of message on an answering machine during the holidays. But I knew it was just another answer to my prayers. My eyes filled with tears as I looked up and thanked God. How awesome is he!

Christmas came and went. We were hopeful that the new year would be a good one. It seemed as if we were turning the corner, but Joey didn't seem enthusiastic. He wasn't himself. I could see stress all over his face. He wasn't happy. When I asked him about it, he told me that he just couldn't get away from it all. He was more miserable than he had ever been in his life. He admitted that he had been throwing up at work every day. I didn't like finding out just how bad it was. I had a stomach ulcer and had taken medication very frequently throughout our ordeal. I knew what it was like. I hated to see him going through it too. The sad thing was that it made me sink lower. We were usually there for each other; one would be strong when the other one wasn't. I didn't feel that I could handle it that time. I wasn't strong enough to carry us both. Truthfully there was a little resentment, because I didn't want to. I wanted things to be okay! What a mess. Shouldn't we just walk away if it's going to affect our health so poorly? Shouldn't we just close the doors and file bankruptcy? But weren't we almost there? Weren't better days finally within our reach? At that point, were better days really even possible?

Joey was upset because things had been happening in the plant. Equipment constantly needed to be repaired. We didn't have the resources available to fix things correctly. We were using "band–aids," as he put it. He had to deal with the quality issues from our recent mouse pad disaster. He was just so tired, and it was becoming very evident.

He also had employee issues to deal with. When we started our business, we weren't received positively by our previous employer. He had signed a non–compete agreement when he sold his company—the one that later closed down and left us unemployed. He opened another business, but this one did blow molding instead of injection molding. He and Joey had a conversation early on. He told Joey that he wouldn't bother any of our employees if we didn't bother any of his. He had a disagreement with one of his customers, who then chose to pull his business and send it to us. We did not go after this business, but we could hardly turn it down either. We needed it. We needed it if we were going to survive. We had recently taken it on. I did wonder what the ramifications would be.

Maybe it was coincidental! Shortly after that, two of our employees turned in their notice. They had been approached by our previous employer and wooed away. We had nothing glamorous to counter–offer. We lost a supervisor and technician from our first shift at the same time. They left immediately following the Christmas holiday. They were our two most knowledgeable people on that shift. What's the saying? If life hands you lemons, make lemonade. We could always use a cut in payroll. We decided to replace them at lower pay and benefit from it if at all possible. We both knew that the success of our business could not solely depend on our employees. We knew that people would come and go over the years. It was, however, additional stress for Joey, as if he needed any.

A couple of weeks went by, and we were both struggling to keep a positive outlook. We were on edge. I was irritable. We had to try to carry on a normal life, at least for our children's sakes. Most of our family really didn't know what we were going through anyway. Talking about it didn't do it justice. Our church friends knew some things. We frequently asked for prayers. There comes a point when you feel like everyone is probably tired of hearing about it. Our friends were great, though. They kept us going a lot of times.

One special couple helped us out tremendously. Wouldn't you know that the first time we did not get the money in time to make payroll would be Christmas week. The thought of telling people they would not get a paycheck made us sick. One of our friends had told us that he would be there if we ever needed him. The last thing we ever wanted to do was to take money from a friend, but we had no choice. We were ten thousand dollars short. That couple gave us a cashier's check for the money in order to make our payroll. Of course, we returned the money as soon we received the check we had been waiting on, but there was still an initial risk. How many people would do that? They did it twice before all was said and done.

Once again our Christian family had come through for us. That added to our depression, though. The whole experience was just so humbling. I was tired of feeling like I had begged everyone in the entire world for money. We had to swallow our pride because it wasn't just us that we had to think about. It was all of our people.

On a good note, one of our customers walked in our office out of the blue and told Joey he wanted to donate one thousand dollars for our Christmas party. We were quite surprised and shocked. We asked him if he minded if we used the money to give to our employees as a bonus instead of having a party. He thought that was a good idea. To my knowledge, he had no way of knowing our financial situation. That would be our third Christmas, and we had never been able to give our employees bonuses. We had enough to give each one fifty dollars, excluding ourselves. I placed fifty–dollar bills inside of each Christmas card and handed them out with great pleasure.

One lady later thanked Joey and told him that the money had really made a difference. One of her grandchildren would not have gotten much for Christmas, and because of her bonus, she was able to help. Fifty dollars had made a difference. I'm sure quite a few of them had similar stories. None of them knew how close we came to not making payroll that

Christmas, or any of the times before, as far as we knew.

I bought Joey a small gold cross pendant and chain for Christmas. He had given me one, and I thought it was fitting that he have one too. He had left it on the bathroom counter while he was showering and getting ready for church one Sunday morning two weeks after New Year's. Our boys frequently came in and disrupted things before we would ask them to leave. I noticed that Alex had the chain in his hand. Then I noticed that the cross was gone. We quickly looked for it but couldn't find it. We had to leave for church.

When we returned, I made the comment to myself, "Lord if you're still with us, help me find the cross." That wasn't an unusual thing for me. I was in the habit of talking to God in all circumstances in my life. I briefly pondered the symbolism in that statement. I went to the trashcan under our bathroom sink and turned it upside down. I rummaged through the garbage a little, and there lying on the floor was the shiny gold cross. I cleaned up the mess, put the cross on the counter, and went on my way.

Joey was just getting around to taking down the Christmas lights outside that day. When he came back inside, he told me he had found something. Lying on the kitchen counter was another cross. In a clump of dirt, on our sidewalk, was a diamond cross pendant and broken gold chain. I remembered my statement, and my eyes filled with tears once again.

I recognized the necklace. One of our best friends had given her daughter a diamond cross necklace when she had been baptized. She was a teenage girl and hadn't been to my house in a while. She hadn't even told her mother that the cross was missing. She had no idea where she had lost it. She was thrilled to learn that it had been found. We suspected that her mother didn't know because we had not known, so I gave it to her in private. I wanted to share the rest of the story with her mother, but I couldn't.

I did tell Joey what I had asked God. He told me that he also had been praying while taking down the lights. We couldn't just write those things off as coincidences. God had told us over and over again that he *was* with us. What more did we need? We had learned the true meaning of *trust*. We knew we were going to be okay. How magnificent our God is! So we would go back to work on Monday and continue to take one day at a time.

# FACING REALITY

I quickly finished December's financial statements because I was eager to get them to East Texas Regional Development. They had requested to see another month of positive numbers. Thankfully, December was another positive month. Regretfully, we had lost more money than you would think possible in the two and a half years we had been in business! Still, November and December were profitable. I e–mailed the information, very hopeful that I would get a positive response. I was told that the board would meet again in February. We would be discussed; however, popular consensus was that they might want to see six months of positive income. Six months! We were hardly able to get the raw materials we needed to keep up with the growing business. We kept saying we wouldn't make it six more months without help.

But I reminded myself how many times we had said that before. God was continuously helping us. I knew we could still make it without the loan, if it was his will. It sure wouldn't be comfortable, but it was still possible. I knew in my heart that if not for God, we would have closed down long before. I knew that it just didn't matter. If we lost the business, if we lost everything, it was meant to be. I knew God had a plan, as he always had. Neither Joey nor I wanted to be outside the will of God.

> Do not be anxious about anything, but in everything, by prayer and petition, with thanksgiving, present your requests to God. And the peace of God, which transcends all understanding, will guard your hearts and your minds in Christ Jesus.
>
> Philippians 4:6–7

I had found peace that transcends understanding. I had learned to be thankful for the things that were going well in my life.

I went on a ladies' retreat one weekend with my church. I sat quiet and still, staring at a lady who had enough courage to stand before us and tell us about the tragedies in her life. She had overcome a battle with cancer in her young adult walk. The doctors had told her to get her affairs in order. She survived and decided to have children. She then lost a toddler child in an explosion at her home, and her husband was badly burned. Her father passed away from cancer on the day her second child was born. I wanted to scream at her to stop. I wanted to go off in a room and cry. She stood strong and showed us how to let our lights shine. How could I feel sorry for myself and my situation?

I was truly blessed with a husband, two healthy children, and a wonderful church family. Though we had lost an enormous amount of money, we had somehow made every payroll, kept up with the taxes, and paid every credit card payment on time. That was a miracle in itself, so when February came and the board decided they would not think about helping us until July, I took it with a grain of salt. There were no dramatics that time, no punches to the stomach. The board members weren't deciding our fate. They weren't the ones in control, and I knew it.

One month went by, then another. We were still there. Somehow we were surviving. There still was no room for comfort, but cash flow had improved a little bit. Our bottom line gradually continued to improve. We had finally reached the turning point. July was our three-year mark for the business. I had looked forward to July so that we could go back to ETCOG and get the loan. For the past six months we had been making partial payments toward large outstanding debts to several of our vendors. They were growing more and more frustrated as time went on.

One day in July we were struck by lightning— literally. Joey walked into our computer room after five one afternoon, after everyone had gone for the day, and smelled something burning. There had been a bad storm, one of several days of repeated storms. Lightning had struck the wiring that went to our phone system and all of our computers including the server. Things were a mess for a few days, but we were pretty fortunate. None of our data had been lost. We were able to transfer information to a borrowed computer temporarily. Our phone service person was able to get two lines out of four working for a few days. We were able to keep things up–to–date in our borrowed computer. Eventually every computer would have to be replaced once we received the check from the insurance company. It could have been far worse, but nevertheless it was just another situation to be dealt with on top of constant equipment repairs, employee turnover, and lack of money.

When July had come and gone, I hurriedly completed the financial statements and sent them to ETCOG. I had a good feeling this time for sure. We had made it six months. We had proven that things were turning around. While we were waiting to hear from them, we were contacted by a competitor of ours.

There was a company in Fort Worth that had been bought by some investors, and they were looking to continue expanding. We had actually taken some business from this company, thus we were of interest to them. They also liked our location. We agreed to meet with them, though I was somewhat reluctant. I was aware that businesses usually were purchased based on their worth. Ours was negative. I also wasn't exactly excited about the idea of selling the company. Joey was. He was so tired of fighting the cash flow problem. Every decision he made had to be driven by the money factor.

Besides the stress I dealt with in paying bills and making payroll, I still loved my job. Being self–employed was my dream. I had visions of my children one day running the business. I had been so blessed the past three years with being able to spend a lot of time with my children and still receive a paycheck. I made sure I had my job done, and I worked hard, but I came and went as I pleased when my children had something I wanted to attend. I had lost my babysitter over the summer and was able to keep the boys myself much of the time. I was pretty sure I would never have a job like that again. Our boys loved visiting Mommy and Daddy's office. I would stop and get them a treat. They would sit at the table in the break room with their snacks and draw pictures. They got to visit their Mamaw there as well. Mamaw would let them copy their little hands on the copy machine.

But my husband was miserable, so I agreed to have an open mind. We met, and even after learning of our debt, they still requested additional information. So we gave them what they wanted and waited for a response.

The meeting had gone well, much to my surprise. They talked about purchasing our business based on our forecast over future months and not the past. Joey and I discussed the possibilities and my reluctance. I told him that I hated to see us turn it over to someone when we had finally begun to do better. We had endured so much over the past three years not to get anything out of it. Joey was hoping to eliminate the debt and move on. I tried to reason that our cash flow would be steadily improving with the new business we were expecting. One of our largest customers had just awarded us a new project that was going to increase our sales significantly. They took a discount and paid in ten days. I received a check every Monday like clockwork. I also reminded him that we had the ETCOG loan that should be approved. I was optimistic about the future of our company.

Joey felt strongly that we needed additional resources to make the business successful. He still felt that we were in danger of losing everything at any time. The stress was taking its toll on him. It was a problem every time we needed raw materials. We were always cutting it close. Being the stubborn one, I just hated to give up. I continued to pray that

God would let me know somehow when it was time to let go.

The following week was a payroll week. The check I had counted on like clockwork did not come in. I thought maybe it was delayed in the mail, so I waited for Tuesday. It didn't come on Tuesday either. So I called the company and asked if they had sent us a check. They told me that their corporate office had instructed them not to take discounts any more. They were going to start paying in forty–five days. This was disappointing to me, but I was still okay.

The next day I received a letter in the mail from ETCOG. Not even a phone call. They regretted to inform us that the board decided against the loan, again. I was surprised and frustrated, but I was *still* okay. I could plainly see the changes that God had made in me over the past three years. I no longer fell apart at the sign of trouble. Payroll was Friday and we had no money. I ran the checks anyway and just prayed about it as I always had.

Thursday afternoon, one of our customers walked in the door and paid on his account. It was enough to pay everyone but one of ourselves. That was typical. It had happened many times before. The point is, that three years into this thing we still didn't know if we would make payroll until the day it was due. Joey was tired of living on the edge. I saw it as proof once again that God was providing.

The preacher asked in his sermon the next Sunday if we were in awe of God. I was! I knew how awesome he really was. I do not believe that any of these things that happened in our business were coincidental. However, it seemed that all of the reasons that I had given to keep going were being discounted in one week! Was God telling me something?

Joey and I agreed to wait it out. There really was no use in getting anxious before we heard what the investors had to say. They could very easily tell us they had decided not to make an offer. That was what I was expecting anyway. I thought it would be a miracle if they offered us enough money to pay off everything in our name. There was no other way it would be beneficial to us.

Although sales had improved and so had our bottom line, you could not tell it by the cash flow. Our situation even seemed worse, if that was possible. We had come to the point that we were forced to pay for raw materials before we could order any new materials. Prior to that we had been purchasing on credit and sending money as we could. I had always managed to pay payroll taxes on time, and I found myself having to put them off. That only causes you to pay penalties, which means more money. I was very upset when the SBA payment was automatically withdrawn from our account and caused us to have insufficient funds. We had always somehow managed to have it covered before. Truthfully it would have been covered then as well if our customer had given us our check on time. We had an agreement with them to pay on the first Thursday of the month. They always did, except for this time. They paid one day late. Our bank luckily covered everything, so nothing was returned, but we did get hit with insufficient funds charges. Then there were all of those finance charges for all of the credit card purchases. We couldn't pay other bills for having to pay those. I routinely made the credit card payments that were due every Monday. So many of them were in our name, and I didn't want our credit ruined. It takes money to make money, and it takes money to save money.

I had been trying so hard for three and a half years to hold things together. More and more I felt like we were drowning. We couldn't breathe. We met with one of the potential investors again. He came to see us and wanted to make sure we were all on the same page before they drew up a letter of intent. It was pretty hard to believe, but they agreed to pay the outstanding debt in our name and incorporate our payables into their own so that they would be paid. They wanted us both to stay on and have Joey be the general manager. Of course, my job would have to be determined. The financial person usually doesn't fare too well in these things.

We would have a small percentage of owner-ship in the new company; small meaning around 2 percent. They were planning to consolidate us with some other companies they were also purchasing, which meant we may or may not be at our current location. They weren't at liberty to tell us where we may end up. The most probable location would be Jacksonville, an hour away. I didn't think that was an option for me. I had no intention of being that far away from my children on a daily basis.

When the man left, it looked as though this were really going to happen. I was not at all excited about it because to me it was the lesser of two evils. The only thing I wanted less than selling to them was going under. But I saw my husband being beaten up almost daily. He came home tired, physically and mentally exhausted. All he could think about was having to return the next day like it was a fate worse than hell itself. He was so miserable. I knew I had no choice. It looked as if God was telling me it was time to give up too. I kept trying to believe that God could pull us out of it at any time and make it all better. I knew he could. But realistically I had finally started to think that it wasn't going to happen. It had gone too far to turn back. Without money, we couldn't even grow. Money wasn't just going to fall out of the sky.

Not long after our meeting, we were running out of material and had nowhere to get it. We were in one of the all-too-common desperate situations. No one would sell it to us because we were so overextended. In a minute of desperation, Joey called his acquaintance from the other company that had been purchased by the investors. He agreed to sell us some of his. Joey let him know that we might not make it if the deal didn't progress more quickly. I have to admit that I was unhappy with my husband at that time. At that point, he wanted out. He didn't care how it happened as long as it happened quickly.

The next meeting was called, and we were asked to meet them halfway. That was the first sign of trouble. We weren't quite sure what to expect at this meeting. Our discussion during the drive was not a lighthearted one. Joey had decided for the most part that we had no choice but to accept what they offered. He believed they were going to ask us to file bankruptcy against the business and let them pick it up on the courthouse steps. I was so, so angry that things had taken that turn. If he had just not let them know how desperate we were. It had been so close to being a done deal. Again, it was never what I wanted in my heart, but I had accepted it was going to be. I prayed all the way to Terrell. I knew it was in his hands and out of mine. I felt I had no choice but to do what the three gentlemen we were meeting and my husband wanted me to do. I told him he would have to send a miracle if things were to be different.

We met at a restaurant and ate first. Then there was the usual small talk that I hated. I just wanted to get down to business. They obviously didn't. They had to bring up the subject lightly. They had decided that it didn't make as much sense after closer inspection to do all of the things they had initially offered. They showed us projections and this and that, and talked in circles and explained it all. When they were finished, my mouth opened. I had prayed that God would help me control my tongue because that is one of my greatest weaknesses. I didn't want to embarrass my husband in front of these men. However, I was his business partner as well as his wife.

They miraculously didn't ask us to file bankruptcy. They just offered to purchase our assets from the bank and wanted us to negotiate our personal debt as far down as we could. They offered their services to help with these creditors. In a nutshell it meant that our credit would still be ruined. Joey's argument with me beforehand was that at least our personal credit would be saved. So when I understood that it would be destroyed anyway, I couldn't seem to help myself. I let them know that I felt their change of heart was directly related to the phone call from Joey, which they denied, at which I laughed. I apologized that they had been misled. Our situation had been desperate for the past three and a half years. Nothing was different. We had no intention of giving up. If they wanted us to go down, we would go down on our own.

To my surprise, Joey agreed. He backed me one hundred percent. We let them know that our name and our credit were important to us. They had approached us. Not the other way around. If we were of interest to them, as they had initially said, they would have to do what they initially offered. After all, they had seen our financial statements and all of the information they requested and still made the offer. Nothing had changed. They just got a glimpse of desperation and thought they would try to get us for nothing. I didn't blame them; I just let them know we knew.

The men sat across from me and told us that if we kept going, we would fail. That really was the wrong thing to say. They obviously didn't know how stubborn I was. It only made me more determined. We ended the meeting with polite smiles and hand-shakes and parted ways.

Joey and I drove home not having a clue which way things would go then. I was determined, but I had started facing the facts that were staring me in the face. I knew how bad things looked and how bad things were. This deal may have been the best thing for us, and I had just told them off. I was afraid

Joey would be mad at me, but he wasn't. We actually agreed on what I had said. If our option was to have our credit ruined and give them everything, why give them everything? We could have our credit ruined on our own and go down fighting.

# GOD IS WITH US

Shortly after that meeting, we got a phone call from one of our customers, a lady Joey dealt with frequently. She knew we were having difficulties. She had some acquaintances who might be able to help. They were investors, and she asked us to meet with them. We thought we might as well. What did we have to lose? They came to our office and met with us in the conference room. They were an odd pair.

One guy was an older man with long hair, a suit jacket, and tennis shoes. The other gentleman wore cowboy boots and a hat. Both men were very friendly. They were good Christian people. We were honest with them and explained the entire situation. The conversation quickly turned to the Lord. Before we knew it, we were holding hands and praying. Tears were flowing from our eyes, all of our eyes! They told us they felt God in that room. They told us that he was with us and not to give up.

After we dried our eyes, we all stood around looking at each other in amazement. What in the world had just happened? If ever I felt like God had sent an angel to our side in a time of need, it was then. Nothing came out of that meeting as far as a business venture, but it meant more to Joey and me than I can say. We hugged the gentlemen before they left and felt like we had made lifetime friends. Sometimes you want God to literally talk to you and tell you you're going to be okay. We felt like he had done just that! I continued to cry after they left. A part of me felt like they were telling us that the business was still going to make it because they said we would be okay.

Low and behold, things immediately started improving. We won the lottery and all of our problems were solved! The business grew beyond our wildest dreams, and we lived happily ever after. That was supposed to be the ending for this story. Because of our prayers and faithfulness, the Lord rewarded us by saving our business. Of course, that is not true. There was still a little hope left in me and then ...

Then my dad called and told us that we were in the newspaper. Elite Plastics, Ltd., Joey and Reneé Meaux, were being sued by a company for nonpayment. We had not even been notified yet, but there it was for all the rest of the world to see. I didn't know it worked like that, but apparently it did.

A few days later, when an older man in the starched white shirt, white cowboy hat, and boots walked in the office and asked to see Joey and me, we knew what he was there for. We were being served. We had been sued. At least that wasn't a surprise, I guess. It was still humiliating. The whole thing was sickening. I was angry. I had certainly prayed against that very thing, not to be sued. If it were God's will to close down the business, couldn't he at least have spared us some shame? Then I remembered once again, my brother–in–law had died. I thought about that often during our journey. I used it to keep reminding myself that our prayers are not always answered the way we want them to be, but that doesn't mean God is not there.

With this latest incident I heard it loud and clear. It was time to quit. However, it was as we had said it would be. We had not given up. There was no choice. I hated the fact that we had come so far in sales that it actually looked like we could make it. We had gone from $700,000 in sales in 2004 to $1,300,000 in sales in 2005. We were so close. I also hated the fact that we actually thought we had miraculously been sent someone to save us just in the nick of time. These things did cause me much confusion and turmoil inside. We were being sued, and the only counteraction we could take was to file bankruptcy. We knew we would lose. We owed the money but had no way to repay it. They could even garnish our personal checking accounts to get the money if we didn't stop them. There it was: the writing on the wall. I saw no other way out. I knew it was over.

We had still been talking with the company that wanted to take us over. They were having problems getting financing, so their plans had been put on hold. Joey and I discussed it at length and prayed at length. We then came up with what we thought was the best plan and our only option.

We met with the company again and told them things had changed. We were done and wanted out. Talk about a humbling experience. We knew our customers would have to transfer to somewhere else. There was a strong likelihood that they would go where Joey went. We told them that he would go to work for the company that made him the best offer. We would file bankruptcy and eliminate the debt. They would not have to pay anything for the business. They could purchase assets if they wanted.

They, in turn, did make him an outstanding offer. So we had one problem taken care of. Joey would have a job, and we would still be taken care of financially. However, closing down our business and filing bankruptcy was the worst thing in the world that could happen to us, I thought. Joey and I had both been such responsible people. We took a lot of pride in our commitments and always carried through. We had acquired more debt in our name than we could ever pay back.

I had been praying all along for God's will to be done and not mine. I knew that was what I was supposed to do. But to be honest, what I truly believed with all my heart was that if I prayed hard enough, our business would succeed. I believed that because we went to God in prayer many times before we even started the business, that the business would be successful. I also thought our prayers could keep my brother–in–law alive. After all, that's what the scripture says, isn't it? "If you believe, you will receive whatever you ask for in prayer" (Matthew 21:22).

I believed. In fact, I had no doubt. God was sure to reward my faith. I told Joey and I told Jack, *Don't give up. The Lord can do anything.* It turned out to be the most humiliating, embarrassing, degrading time of my life. I can't even find the words to describe it. Does God really promise to give us everything we ask for if we believe? No, I don't believe he does.

If you read the context in which that verse was written, Jesus was talking to his disciples. He had given them the power to perform miracles on his behalf to spread the gospel and increase the number of the saved. What a painful lesson to learn. We don't always get what we want.

All of these happenings hurt my feelings and my pride greatly. I had grown to love Jack as family. He worked hand–in–hand with Joey. He was more than a good employee. He knew exactly what our situation was the entire three and a half years, and he had stayed. We had some wonderful supervisors and other employees that I cared for very much, one of whom was my mother. We had to tell them all that it was over. We would have to pack our things and move out of the office that we had designed and decorated. We had to leave it all behind, everything we had fought so hard for. We were losing it all, including the one thing we'd inherited from Joey's father, his home.

We had to tell our partners/investors that they were losing everything as well. That was unbearable. We had been married in their backyard. Needless to say, our relationship would now be strained. That night at home I was overcome with grief and emotion. I tried to put my frustration to use and relieve some stress by exercising. I couldn't find the energy to do it. I sat down on the floor and just cried. I asked God to put his arms around me. I needed him so much. Seconds later my four–year–old child came up the stairs and saw me. He put both of his little arms around me and hugged me tightly. What a blessing it was. I knew what it felt like to be hugged by God! God is with us. He knows our needs and many times shows us his love through people around us. He comforts us in our times of despair. "The Lord is close to the brokenhearted and saves those who are crushed in spirit" (Psalm 34:18).

I remember praying one night while driving to town. I asked God to please expedite things. I understood that we had somewhere else he wanted us to be, and I asked him to show us mercy and hurry up and put us there! We just wanted to move on to the next stage of our lives, whatever that may be.

We went to see an attorney and started the bankruptcy proceedings. We informed our customers that we were closing down, as well as our employees. Then things started moving so quickly it made my head spin. News traveled fast that we were closing. Two very distinguished–looking people came in the office and asked to see me. They sat in front of me in my two burgundy oxford chairs that I was soon to leave behind and explained to me who they were. They were attorneys working for the city of Gladewater. We owed property taxes for 2005 and now 2006—it was January 2006—and they had to be paid or they would file a motion to seize our property and have padlocks placed on our doors. They were afraid we would leave in the middle of the night and they would not get paid. I sat and looked at them across my desk and felt an overwhelming feeling of hopelessness.

I explained to them that our business was still in operation. We were trying our best to take care of everything that we could. I mentioned the fact that I had gone to the city for help so that our thirty–three employees would not have to lose their jobs and we could continue to pay our bills. They refused, but they were the first ones to show up with their hands out when they heard we were closing. I guess they felt sorry for me.

Somehow I convinced them to give me a couple of days. After they left I called my attorney. She told me that they could actually do what they said. She advised me to come up with the taxes for 2005 and pay them. That was more than five thousand dollars. Somehow I was able to take them a check that same day and appease them for a little while longer. Nothing like that had crossed my mind before they came. Suddenly I had to deal with fear along with all of the other emotions.

We needed to close down in our own timing. We had not made the final payroll. We needed the customers' transfer of molds to be a smooth and timely transition so as to not interrupt production. We had a lot of loose ends to tie up. Every night when I left my office, I was afraid that I would not be able to get back in the next day. I knew I needed to take home my personal belongings, but that was difficult for me. I really didn't want any of these things to be happening. I really didn't want to leave. All of a sudden I felt like a criminal in what used to be "our" place. I had no idea what would happen next.

In another ironic turn of events, our previous boss's non–compete agreement had expired. He was moving back into the building across the street from us as we were moving out. I actually found a little relief in the fact that our employees might be able to find work with him. It was another example of God's perfect timing, not a coincidence. Our employees were a great matter of concern for me. I cared about their well–being very much.

By the end of January, all of our employees in the plant had left. It was very hard to tell them good-bye. Jack stayed for a couple of weeks to help close things out. Of course, I cried the day he left. Then my mother, Joey, and I were the last three standing. We told Mom she could go, but she insisted on stay-ing, even if we couldn't pay her. Thankfully, we had some receivables coming in. Since we didn't have to try to buy more raw materials, we could pay some bills. We were able to pay everyone their final checks along with any accrued vacation. We were able to pay all of the local and smaller vendors we owed. We were able to leave with our heads held up, if only just a little.

Along with the plethora of other emotions I had to deal with was the immense feeling of guilt I had because of the people we were not able to pay back. We were walking away from thousands of dollars of debt from our banknote, from vendors, and most importantly to me, from my mother. I prayed fervently that God would somehow help me to pay her back what we had borrowed from her. How in the world would we ever do that? I had no idea how that would be possible, yet I prayed for it anyway. I also felt somewhat guilty because it had been me who was sure the business was going to make it. It was me who drove Joey to keep going when he wanted out.

Time went on as it always does. Joey immediately started working for the other company, which happened to be in Fort Worth, a two–and–a–half–hour drive away. The "great deal" turned out to be too good to be true. They wound up paying him half what we had discussed. Once again, another letdown. We'd had nothing in writing, but the way things had progressed, we had no choice but to take the offer anyway. I was unemployed and staying home with the boys. I knew there was a reason things turned out the way they did. I certainly had no idea what it was. I prayed that God might reveal that to us one day. But nothing had turned out as I had hoped or prayed for, or had it?

I had prayed for his will to be done. I knew we were where he wanted us to be. I knew no matter how much it hurt, he was giving me the strength to get through it.

Joey had to travel to Fort Worth a few days a week in the beginning. After that he got to work out of our house. We set up an office upstairs. I quickly saw a change in him. The weight had finally been lifted off his shoulders. I don't think he ever went through a mourning period. It was instant relief for him. It was a huge change going from the stress of running our business to working out of our house. A change he greatly needed and appreciated.

I soon found out that it was kind of nice to be unemployed and a stay–at–home mom. The bankruptcy included all of our personal debt as well as the company's. That was the way it had to be done because so much of the credit was in our name. So all of our personal debt was eliminated with the exception of our house and vehicles. Could it be that we were actually financially better off? I had not chosen that route. In fact, we had tried our best to avoid that route. It seemed strange that we had, in a way, benefited from it. The worst possible thing in the world that could happen, turned out not to be so bad after all. We were still alive and well. We still had our family and our health. We could finally breathe.

Things weren't so great for my mother. She was able to draw unemployment, but it was a cut in pay. Her inheritance was gone. She and my dad would have to make it off of their Social Security. I helped them as much as I could.

Jack temporarily found work with his brother–in–law in the oilfield business. Before that he drew unemployment for a while. His mother–in–law was terminally ill and needed care around the clock. Jack was able to stay with her when she needed it most. We got to see him when his son got married and again at his mother–in–law's funeral. We knew we would be a part of each other's lives now forever.

We saw John, our third shift supervisor, in a restaurant one night. He had a good job that he really liked. It was great to see him and find out that he was doing well.

A few of our employees would call occasionally and keep in touch. It brought tears to my eyes to talk to them, but it was wonderful to know that most of them were doing okay. Everybody just moved on. I had felt such a responsibility to take care of them all.

I remember one employee named Glenn. Glenn's girlfriend moved out of his apartment and took all of their belongings with her. He was left with an empty apartment that he could no longer afford on his own. The first thing he had to let go of was the electricity. It was Christmastime, our last Christmas there. The days and nights were cold. He was sleeping on the floor of a cold, damp, dark apartment for a while, and then he got evicted. We put him in a motel and paid for him to stay there for a week until he could make other arrangements. We invited him to our home for Christmas Eve, but he didn't come. We, along with our boys, took him lots of food, cookies, and candy that night and enjoyed the true spirit of Christmas. That was a blessing for all of us. I also discovered that my mother was bringing him lunch every day. It may just have been a tuna fish sandwich or something, but she made sure he had something to eat. When we closed down, Glenn moved out of town to live with family.

# A NEW SEASON

I had no idea what the future had in store for me. I told God that I had no idea and I was exhausted. I told him he would have to bring it to me, whatever it was that he wanted me to do. I loved my independence and was really kind of sad about the idea of being a full–time employee again. I thought I might know what God wanted for me. What could be better than having my own business?

Yes, I was going to do it again! But this time, it was going to be *my* own business. I was going to start my own accounting business and work out of my office at home too. I had acquired invaluable experience. After all, I knew how to start a business and I knew how to shut one down! I ran one on a dime for three and a half years. I had every confidence that the failure of our business was not due to lack of experience or expertise on either my or Joey's part. It was lack of capital, plain and simple. I have read that it takes a new business a good three years to turn the corner, and we actually had. I have also read that businesses close down due to lack of capital more than any other reason. A business out of my home with no other employees would require very little overhead. I wouldn't need a great amount of resources. What a great idea! I could employ my mother eventually and help her too.

I put the plan in motion. I couldn't just sit around feeling sorry for myself and doing nothing. I had brochures and business cards printed up. I advertised in the newspaper. I sent out letters to previous contacts I had made. There I was, on my way. There was definitely a pattern of me trying to fix things.

"Be still before the Lord and wait patiently for him" (Psalm 37:7). God had other plans for me. Mark, the man I had gone to work for briefly before Joey and I started our company, heard that we had closed the business. Mark had run into a mutual friend of ours and asked her to pass on the word for me to call him. I thought about it a couple of weeks before I actually did it. I knew he had replaced me long ago. I picked up the phone, I guess out of curiosity—or was it?

He had started another company since I had left. He needed a financial manager. He asked me to meet him at a coffee shop, so I did. He had two partners; each one had other businesses as well. I explained to him that I was going to start my own business. He said he could keep me busy with all of their work and would like me to work for them exclusively. He offered me a good salary and said he would like me to be in the office at least from nine to three. I would be able to be with my boys after school. He had a suite in the bank building that was ready for me to move into. There wasn't really much to think about. I had acquired all of my clients with one swoop. I accepted the offer and was excited about getting started.

My office was on the third floor of the bank building. It had a large window the entire length of the room. The furniture was ornate and expensive. It was actually supposed to have been Mark's office, but they had changed their plans. There was a flat-screen TV mounted on the wall with a remote control on the desk! I had always wanted a TV in my office, but we couldn't afford the luxury of cable. It was quite prestigious. I have to admit, I felt like a child on Christmas morning.

My first assignment was to decorate! There was no one else working there with me, just me! The plans were for me to get the office ready and then they would move their accounting ladies, who officed in their Kilgore plant, in with me. We would become the corporate office. Mark and the partners had other offices. My contact with them was mostly by phone or e-mail. The first couple of weeks, I was there by myself, in and out, shopping for the new office, spending someone else's money. I had learned to be very frugal, of course.

It really was a dream job. Maybe it wouldn't be for everyone, but it was absolutely wonderful for me. Our past experience had made me really appreciate the simpler things in life. The opportunity literally fell into my lap. It seemed too good to be true, only it wasn't. It was September, and the kids were just going to start school. I was going to quit receiving my unemployment checks. The timing was perfect once again. God knew when I took the job for Mark before we started our endeavor that he was preparing a place for me to come back to. It became very clear to me why I had accepted that job several years before.

When I met the ladies who came to work with me in the new corporate office, I was very pleased. They were Christian ladies. We even prayed together. All three of the partners were Christian men as well. The company tithed from its profits. It helped support many ministries. It was helping to build a children's home in Peru. It was contributing to ministries in India, China, Honduras, and Puerto Rico, among many others around the world. Numerous great things were being done through this company for the work of the kingdom. As the financial manager, my responsibility was to oversee all of the accounting and finances. I have always known that we are supposed to work like we are working for the Lord, but this was the first time I had felt that.

Whatever you do, work at it with all your heart,
as working for the Lord, not for men, since you
know that you will receive an inheritance from
the Lord as a reward. It is the Lord Christ you
are serving.

Colossians 3:23–24

I felt like the keeper of his money. The more
money I could save, the more the company made, the
more substantial a tithe check I got to send out for the
Lord's work. I felt like God wanted me there. He put
me there for a reason. It was part of his plan. It was
absolutely amazing how it all worked out. No matter
what I had done to try to fix things, or what plans I
made for myself, I ended up right where God wanted
me to be. "Many are the plans in a man's heart, but it
is the Lord's purpose that prevails" (Proverbs 19:21).

I felt so blessed and so excited to be on a new
and different journey. I couldn't help but want to
tell everyone what God had done for me. All of my
friends and family had seen the stress that Joey and I
had been under. They could see it written all over our
faces. Now they could see true joy in me. I was and
still am completely in awe of our God.

Joey's new job had been immediate relief for
him. Being able to work from home and on his own
schedule was what he needed at the time. It wasn't
his *dream job*, however. He was very happy for me,

but he commented one day that he wished he had what I had. He didn't want to work for a company in Fort Worth forever. Joey likes structure. He's not the type to work out of his home continuously. He likes the corporate scene. He fits in very well with the corporate scene. He continued to work for the company we transferred most of our business to for about a year.

Then one day a friend of ours told him of a job opening they were having at the plastics company he worked for. He asked Joey if he'd be interested. It was a local Fortune 100 company. Joey decided to send them his résumé. He was offered the position. He was very pleased with the offer and accepted the job. He now had his ideal job too, and it had come to him as mine had. It was a gift from God. We had not gotten there from any efforts of our own.

The company he left, the one that was going to save us, closed down not long afterward. He had left just in time. I realized that more than likely those men were not able to come through with what they had originally offered. It wasn't due to Joey's showing them our desperation, which had upset me. God has shown me several times since then that things are not always as they seem. I couldn't help but remember what *they* had said to us, that if we kept going *we* would fail.

Joey's new associates were also Christian people. He was a project manager and had been promoted very quickly after taking the job. He reported to people in a different location as well. We were both grateful for the little sense of liberation that brings after managing your own business.

We are not rich in the monetary terms of the word, but we are comfortable, and we are able to help others. We are happy and content. We are blessed. We may not be at the same companies forever. Only God knows what's in store for the future. If something changes, we were there for a season.

> There is a time for everything, and a season for every activity under heaven: a time to be born and a time to die, a time to plant and a time to uproot, a time to kill and a time to heal, a time to tear down and a time to build, a time to weep and a time to laugh, a time to mourn and a time to dance, a time to scatter stones and a time to gather them, a time to embrace and a time to refrain, a time to search and a time to give up, a time to keep and a time to throw away, a time to tear and a time to mend, a time to love and a time to hate, a time for war and a time for peace.
>
> Ecclesiastes 3:1–8

I don't worry about whether this job will end. I'm sure it will, when the time comes. If it does, the Lord will provide.

I truly believe the same is true for the three and a half years of struggling we went through. We were there for a season. We were there for a purpose. We touched lives in ways that we may never even know. *Our* lives were touched by the employees and other people we came to know during that time. I believe we were there exactly as long as God wanted us to be and then no more. As I said before, our previous employer moved back in across the street, literally as we were moving out. We were there just long enough to keep some of the people employed until he returned.

Though it seemed like hell, the experience was invaluable for us both, career–wise as well as spiritually. Never had we been more dependent on God. I recounted some of the situations where I could see God's hands in our business very clearly keeping us going when we thought there was no hope.

It's very difficult for me to express the feelings and repercussions of not knowing until Thursday or Friday morning if I would actually be able to give our employees their paychecks that were due that day. We didn't need a few hundred dollars to make payroll, we needed thousands. The entire time was full of what I believe were miracles. I am so blessed to be a part of that! There *is* a God! He is so faithful in keeping his promises to take care of us.

I stayed in my office in the bank building working nine to three for one year. It was wonderful to be with my boys after school. Then they asked me to move the office back in with the plant located in Kilgore and work from eight to five. I was a little sad at first and prayed that it wouldn't happen, but it did. The plant in Kilgore was an empty building when Joey and I started our business. We had actually looked at it on our quest to find a building for ourselves. Ironically, I ended up working there for someone else.

Because of the extra hours, I received an increase in pay. I had been working on repaying my parents what I owed them. I gave them my increase in salary monthly, and though it's not without difficulty, my mother hasn't had to go back to work yet. God is providing.

I found that I still loved my job and even more, the people I work for and with. My employers are very flexible in allowing me to attend school functions or things that involve my kids. Joey is so obviously much happier.

Our two boys are now seven and nine years old. They are going from baseball to football to basketball almost year–round. Joey coaches their teams and is secretary of the White Oak Baseball Association.

Last year he was the tee ball commissioner; however, our tee–baller has moved up. Joey remains a deacon in our church and helps to oversee the children's ministry. He is not a slave to the business any more. I am not a slave to the guilt any more.

I truly believe God used even my stubbornness as a tool to accomplish his plan. I have no doubt that we did everything within our power for that business. If there was any place else in this country to look for help, I wasn't aware of it. There was no government bailout for us. I prayed continually that the Lord would make it clear to me when it was time to go because I could not quit on my own. He did. I have no regrets.

# ALL FOR HIS GLORY

We are enjoying our new lives without the stress. We never even looked back once it finally came to an end. That was a very pleasant surprise. We just felt tremendous relief. We are certified scuba divers and are now able to travel. We take regular cruises and vacations searching for new places to dive. God has blessed us with discovering the world beneath the sea.

I will never forget the first time we dove the reefs in Cozumel, Mexico. It was truly a spiritual experience for me. The colors of the coral and the fish were absolutely breathtaking. Seeing sharks can also take your breath away. We have seen a couple of those. Joey absolutely loves the thrill. I pray continuously. It never stops being a little scary, but you soon get lost in the magnificence of it all. How could anyone see the brilliance, the majesty of this earth, and not believe in the God who created it?

We were able to take a ten–day cruise around the Hawaiian Islands and dive there as well. Hawaii was my ideal vacation, the place I have always dreamed of going. It was as wonderful as I had thought it would be; paradise on earth. The views are spectacular above and below the ocean.

We have taken our parents on a cruise. I will never forget going up the escalator with my father to board the ship. He said, "I'm so excited!" He had never been able to do anything like that before. What a joy to be able to give that to him and both of our mothers.

We have taken our children on a Disney cruise. I'm not sure who was more excited, them or my father. They have been introduced to snorkeling and do it quite well. The four of us snorkeled off the coast of Disney's private island in the Bahamas in search of buried treasure. I'm sure diving will be a family event also, once they are old enough to be certified.

My father is an avid sports fan, as well as my boys. One of the perks of my new job was being able to take him and all three of my boys, including Joey, to a couple of Texas Ranger games in Arlington. My employers purchased a suite for the season for entertaining customers. Since I was the keeper of the tickets, I was sometimes able to use the leftovers. The suite sat up behind home plate. We had food and drinks catered. It was "sweet," according to my boys. My father actually got to go three times this last season, once just him and his best friend. He thought he had died and gone to heaven. I was delighted to hear the thrill in his voice when I called to see how they were doing. Life has many small pleasures to offer. We have many more places to discover and adventures to embark on, if it be his will.

We will never forget our brief encounter with entrepreneurship. It was a terribly humbling experience. I had to get my husband's approval to share this story because it is his story too. He's a private person. I know it isn't easy for him to share everything.

We were joking about possible titles for a book about our venture. These were his ideas that just about say it all:

1. If You Can Survive Your Own Business, You Can Survive Hell

2. How to Survive Getting Your Guts Ripped Out on a Daily Basis

3. To Hell and Back

4. How to Lose More Money than You've Ever Seen in Your Life

5. The Money Pit

6. Who Can Accumulate the Most Maxed–Out Credit Cards?

7. Business on a Band–Aid

8. Band–Aid Business

9. Lose Money from Day One

10. The Dummy's Guide to Being an Idiot

11. The Dummy's Guide to Losing Money

12. How to Make Yourself Miserable without Even Trying

Yes, these are humorous, but they are also pretty accurate descriptions of what we went through.

The journey was mayhem. I know worse things have happened to people than what happened to us. However, when it's *you* going through it—actually going through it—it doesn't seem like much could be worse. People have committed suicide and murder for less. Though it may appear to some that we were living the American dream because we were self–employed, it was more of an American nightmare. I have learned that if you want what others have, be willing and prepared to do whatever they went through to get it, whether it be years of education or experience. Great achievements seldom come without great responsibility, sacrifice, and risk. Most people just want the end result.

Christians wonder what they have done wrong to be on the receiving end of tribulation. Some people believe their businesses are successful because they are "good" Christians. The truth is that some people of the world are very successful even though they are not Christians. Our business didn't fail because God was not with us. It failed because God had other plans for us.

God works things according to his purpose. It may bring him more glory for a business to be unsuccessful. If it brings God glory, it's not failure. If he closes that door, he will open another one. "For I know the plans I have for you, declares the Lord, plans to prosper you and not to harm you, plans to give you hope and a future" (Jeremiah 29:11).

The world commonly asks, *If there is a God, why does he allow such pain and suffering?* Jesus tells his disciples when they ask him why a certain man was born blind, "Neither this man nor his parents sinned," said Jesus, "but this happened so that the work of God might be displayed in his life" (John 9:3).

I bought a CD one night from a church family member who has an angelic voice. She is a talented songwriter as well. I was very touched with her answer to that same question. The song says, "That the Father's power might be shown, and that the depths of mercy unimagined can be known. It was all for his glory." It goes on to say, "So we can shout there is a God, and my God hears my plea." I listened to that song over and over, and tears welled up in my eyes. I knew I needed to share our story. It *was* all for his glory!

Now that we have been removed from the distressing situation we were in, I still continually pray. I thank the Lord every day for the blessings he has given me. I'm sure there are more trials to be encountered. We are to be grateful for these trials, though it is against human nature. God is more concerned with our character than our comfort.

> And we rejoice in the hope of the glory of God. Not only so, but we also rejoice in our sufferings, because we know that suffering produces perseverance; perseverance, character, and character, hope. And hope does not disappoint us, because God has poured out his love into our hearts by the Holy Spirit, whom he has given us.
>
> Romans 5: 2–5